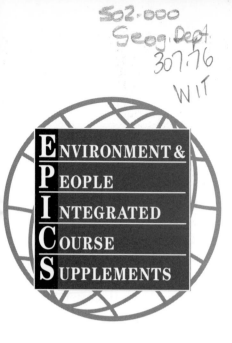

ENVIRONMENT &
PEOPLE
INTEGRATED
COURSE
SUPPLEMENTS

THE URBAN
WORLD

Processes and issues

Michael Witherick

DETUR GLORIA SOLI DEO
1913
Library
Trinity Grammar School
Summerhill 2130

Series Editor:
Michael Witherick

STANLEY
THORNES

Stanley Thornes (Publishers) Ltd

First published in 1999 by:
Stanley Thornes (Publishers) Ltd
Ellenborough House
Wellington Street
CHELTENHAM GL50 1YW
England

00 01 02 03/ 10 9 8 7 6 5 4 3 2

A catalogue record for this book is available from the British Library.

ISBN 0-7487-4419-3

Designed by Giles Davies
Page layout and illustrations by Hardlines,
Charlbury, Oxfordshire
Cover design by Sterling Associates
Printed and bound in Great Britain by Martins the Printers Ltd,
Berwick upon Tweed

Acknowledgements

With thanks to the following for permission to reproduce photographs and other copyright material in this book:

Fotofusion, Fig. 5.9(left)
Sally and Richard Greenhill Photo Library, Fig. 4.1(left)
Hutchison Library, Fig. 5.3
Meadowhall Centre Ltd, Fig. 6.2
Panos Pictures, Fig. 3.5
Safeway Stores plc, Fig. 4.1(right)
Still Pictures, Fig. 5.8

Harper Collins, Fig. 6.4 (from J. Herington, *The Outer City*, Harper & Row, 1984, p.41); Longman Group Ltd, Figs 4.2, 5.7 (from H. Carter, *Urban and Rural Settlement*, Longman, 1990, pages 118 and 135); Oxford University Press, Figs 4.4, 4.5 (from E. Jones and J.Eyles, *An Introduction to Social Geography*, OUP, 1977, page 180); Penguin Books Ltd, Fig. 4.3 (from B. Goodall, *Dictionary of Human Geography*, 1987, page 110); *Times* Syndication, Figs 6.5, 6.8.

Every effort has been made to contact copyright holders. The publishers apologise to anyone whose rights have been inadvertently overlooked, and will be happy to rectify any errors or omissions.

Information was also used from the following sources, to which the author and publishers acknowledge their indebtedness:
Fig.4.8 from S.D. Brunn and J.F. Williams, *Cities of the World*, Harper & Row, 1983, p.188; Fig.6.3 from J.R. Short, *An Introduction to Urban Geography*, RKD, 1996, p.239; and Figs 6.6 and 6.7 from N. Low and D. Smith, *Decision-making Geography*, Stanley Thornes, 1991, p.219.

Contents

CHAPTER

1

From urbanisation to counterurbanisation

SECTION A

Introduction

Of all the human impacts on the face of the Earth, none has been greater and more widespread than the growth of towns and cities. The **urban environment** – that is, the built-up area of a town or city – is largely an artificial environment. It has been made by people for people. It covers and destroys the natural environment. Because towns and cities pollute both air and water, their environmental impact often reaches beyond the built-up area. Once created, the urban environment profoundly affects the way people live, giving rise to life-styles that are quite distinct from those in rural areas.

Today, close to half the world's population of over 6000 million people lives in an urban environment (**1.1**). In 1800 the figure was less than 5 per cent. There are now nearly 300 cities with individual populations greater than 1 million. Whether we like it or not, most of us on this planet now live in an urban world. Furthermore, the rate of urbanisation shows no signs of slowing down; quite the opposite in fact.

Figure 1.1 Global population growth and urbanisation, 1800–2000

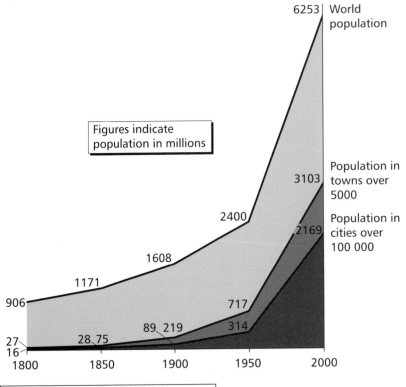

Review

1 Describe what you understand by the term **built-up area**.

2 Explain the following:
   - how towns and cities cover and destroy natural environments
   - the sources of urban pollution
   - why urban pollution often reaches beyond the built-up area.

3 Write a brief analysis of **1.1**.

Basic definitions

The introduction that you have just read contains terms and basic ideas that need to be clearly understood from the outset. This section and the next aim to help you here.

Although the term **urban** is the key one for this book, sadly there is no universally accepted definition. However, most would agree that the idea of people and settlements surviving largely on the basis of non-agricultural activities lies at the heart of the term. In other words, economic activity provides the basis for distinguishing between urban and rural places. An **urban settlement** is one that survives mainly by means of activities like mining, manufacturing goods and providing services. **Rural settlements** are most commonly those relying on farming, but fishing and forestry can also provide a livelihood. Rooted in the term **rural** is the idea of countryside and open space.

Important though economic activity is to the difference between urban and rural, there is also a social dimension. There is an urban way of life or urban life-style (sometimes referred to as **urbanism**). Pace and stress are certainly a feature of that life-style. Urban work is also different: job opportunities are both more varied and greater in number. Success at work can be converted into material possessions and progress up the social scale. Social interaction and upward mobility are not held back by old social structures. Much revolves around what you do for a living and how much you earn. Better services and more leisure opportunities are among the things that help to promote the belief that towns and cities offer a superior quality of life. People probably behave differently in an urban environment. This is suggested by higher rates of crime and other forms of social malaise. Self-interest tends to prevail rather than community care. Urban society is highly polarised: great wealth and acute poverty exist almost side by side.

If urbanism really does exist – and that is questioned by some – we would have to admit that it has now spread beyond the built-up area. City-based mass-media, and the fact that people living in so-called rural areas look to towns and cities for jobs and services, mean that they are drawn increasingly into an urban-based society. The promotion of such a society, with its associated values, perceptions and behaviour, is inevitably diluting rural areas and rural life-styles.

Urban settlements can range enormously in size, from the small and simple to the huge and complex. There is a sequence of terms commonly used to cover this great range. The sequence starts with **town** and is followed by **city** (formerly marked by its functional status in such fields as trade, government and religion). In some studies of urbanisation, the minimum threshold of a town is set at a population of 5000 and that of a city at 100 000 (**1.1**).

The size sequence carries on from city to **metropolis** (the chief city of a state or region), to **conurbation** (a continuous urban area formed by the growing together of once-separate towns and cities) and finally to **megalopolis** (a vast urban area formed by the coalescence of conurbations and cities). This size sequence creates a sort of vertical class system known as an **urban hierarchy**, which may be visualised as a form of pyramid. At its base there are many towns; above these lie a lesser number of cities; above them still fewer metropolitan centres; and so the structure of the system tapers upwards (see **Chapter 2 Section C** and **2.3**).

In each of these different categories of the urban hierarchy, there is a recurring problem – where to draw the limits of the urban area. To put it simply, where does urban settlement end and rural space begin? There are at least two different answers to this question. A **formal** definition states that an urban settlement ends where the physical expressions of its growth – namely the bricks and mortar – give way to green space. In contrast, a **functional** definition states that an urban settlement extends as far out as it draws in labour to fill its jobs and clients for its services. Clearly, the functional definition of a town or city is going to be more generous and extensive. But both definitions have one thing in common: the boundary is not a clear-cut line. Towns and cities have fringes or zones of transition. Here, the type of land use, density of population and character of settlement gradually change from being predominantly urban to predominantly rural. This is the **rural–urban fringe**. Again, a functional rural–urban fringe is wider than one that is defined on the basis of form.

Review

4 Make a list of those things that you think distinguish the urban from the rural way of life.

5 Suggest why population size might not be a sound basis for distinguishing between towns and cities.

6 Draw a diagram to show the structure of an urban hierarchy.

7 Name a town, city, metropolis, conurbation and megalopolis in a country that you have studied.

8 Explain why a functional definition of the rural–urban fringe is likely to be wider than a formal definition.

9 Describe the appearance of an area that you know at first hand and which you would regard as part of the rural–urban fringe.

The nature of urbanisation

This book is all about one process and its spatial outcomes. **Urbanisation** is the process of change by which places and people become increasingly urban. It causes a rise in the percentage of a population living in towns and cities. The percentage of people earning their living from urban activities also increases. These values, along with others, indicate what is known as the **degree** or **level of urbanisation**.

Urbanisation is a multi-strand process. Four changes are particularly important.

- **A shift in the economy** of a region or country, with the emphasis moving from farming and the primary sector to manufacturing and the provision of centralised services. This shift is essential for **development**. Development is the force that drives urbanisation (see **Section D**).
- **A change in the distribution of population**. The spatial concentration of people and their non-agricultural activities at favoured locations leads to the birth and growth of towns and cities. A vital part of this aspect of urbanisation is **rural–urban migration**.
- **A change in the way of life** of those people helping to swell the populations of towns and cities. It is not just a change in occupation; it is a change in life-styles, values, behaviour and social institutions. In short, urbanisation involves the rise and spread of **urbanism**.
- **Changes in the size and character of settlements**. Some settlements, particularly those at favoured locations, grow more quickly than others. Differential growth in the settlement network sees some villages grow into towns, some towns into cities, and so on.

Having identified these four major strands of change, we can begin to realise that urbanisation has other important features.

- It is initially centripetal in character: emerging towns and cities act as magnets drawing in people and activities. As we shall see in **Section F**, that particular characteristic changes as the urbanisation process advances.
- It is a spatial process: it causes places to change.
- It is a process that can operate at a whole range of speeds. In some places it may be very slow and almost imperceptible; in others it can be fast and frightening. The speed is largely conditioned by the overall speed of development in a country or region (see **Section E**).
- It is also a spatial process: at any one time some places will have achieved higher levels of urbanisation than others (**1.5**, **1.6**).

These last two features of urbanisation are particularly important. They need to be explored a little more.

What is known as the **urbanisation curve** is a generalisation based on the experiences of countries around the world (**1.2**). It suggests that with development, countries follow a sequence of urbanisation. Because the curve is S-shaped, the sequence involves four phases.

- **The rural society phase** – although some towns may exist, the level of urbanisation is low and rises only imperceptibly.
- **The take-off phase** – the rate of urbanisation accelerates.

- **The drive-to-maturity phase** – the rate of urbanisation becomes steady, but the overall level of urbanisation continues to rise impressively.
- **The mass-urbanisation phase** – the rate of urbanisation slows, but the level of urbanisation remains high and continues to rise slowly.

However, the sequence may not end there. The recent changes in the most advanced MEDCs* are beginning to suggest that we might extend the urbanisation curve and possibly recognise a fifth phase.

- **The counterurbanisation phase** – the rate of urbanisation levels off and then appears to slip back. Some urban people become disillusioned. They begin to believe that the grass is greener, if not on the rural side of the fence, then certainly outside the big city. Whether the outcome is a decrease in the level of urbanisation is very debatable. We will return to this reversal in **Section F** and **Chapter 6**.

Figure 1.2 The urbanisation curve and stages of urbanisation

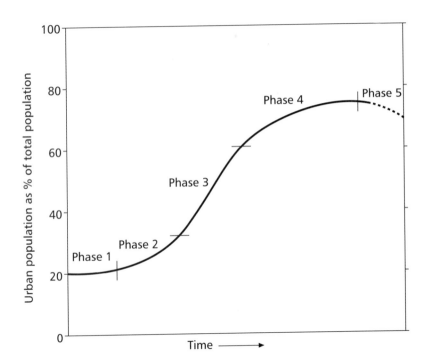

The urbanisation curve is a model largely based on what has happened in the MEDCs (**1.2**). It assumes that most, if not all, of today's LEDCs* will eventually follow the same sequence of changes. That is debatable, but the case becomes more convincing if we make one vital qualification. It is that each country moves along the urbanisation curve at its own pace. There is no fixed time-scale, no fixed rate of progress. For example, it took the UK

*In this book references to the two major global divisions use two sets of interchangeable terms: **the North** and **the South**; and the **more economically developed countries** (**MEDCs**) and the **less economically developed countries** (**LEDCs**). The terms **developed country/world** and **developing country/world** also match the distinction.

over 200 years to complete the four phases, while Japan did so in a quarter of the time. In other words, for some countries, such as the Asian Tigers before the meltdown of the Asian economy in the late 1990s, the urbanisation curve was highly compressed along the time axis. For others, such as the weakest LEDCs, progress will scarcely if ever be anything other than slow. Indeed, there is no guarantee that all the LEDCs will eventually reach the high levels of urbanisation suggested by the model. For these tail-enders, the urbanisation curve will still be S-shaped, but it will be seriously 'flattened' by two things: the slow pace of development, and the persistence of relatively low levels of urbanisation.

So we should imagine the urbanisation curve as a pathway. A snapshot of the global pathway at any particular time will show the countries of the world scattered along it, momentarily 'frozen' as they move along at different speeds. In short, the snapshot will show a significant geographical feature, namely that the level and rate of urbanisation vary from country to country. That point is illustrated by the data in **1.3**. The 15 countries have been organised into five groups which possibly fit with the five phases in **1.2**.

Review

10 Identify the main features of urbanisation.

11 Why is it justifiable to call the urbanisation curve an urban model (1.2)?

12 Describe the economic and social conditions you would expect to be associated with each of the phases on the urbanisation curve (1.2).

	Urban population as % of total			
	1950	1970	1990	2000 est.
Phase 5				
Australia	75	85	86	85
Sweden	66	81	84	83
UK	84	89	93	90
Phase 4				
Brazil	35	56	77	81
Japan	50	71	77	78
South Korea	21	41	72	86
Phase 3				
Greece	37	53	63	68
Mexico	43	59	73	78
Pakistan	18	25	32	38
Phase 2				
China	11	20	21	35
Indonesia	12	17	29	40
Senegal	31	33	40	45
Phase 1				
Ethiopia	5	9	12	15
Uganda	3	6	11	14
Vietnam	12	18	22	22

Figure 1.3
Levels of urbanisation in a sample of countries, 1950–2000

Urbanisation and development

Figure 1.4 The relationship between urbanisation and development in a sample of

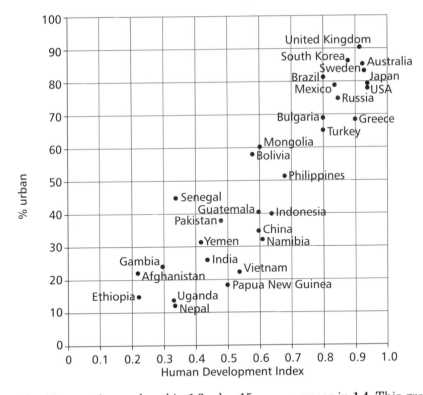

The 15 countries analysed in **1.3**, plus 15 more, appear in **1.4**. This graph seeks to establish whether or not there is a link between urbanisation and the broader development process. Although it is not perfect, the **Human Development Index** provides a fairly sound multi-variate measure of development. The general diagonal spread of the 30 countries across the graph does seem to point to a broad relationship. But what is the exact nature of that relationship? It is highly likely that economic development fuels urbanisation, particularly through the growth of the secondary and tertiary sectors of the economy. Equally, it is also very possible that urbanisation helps promote the more social aspects of development, such as better education, housing and medical services.

The data in **1.5** provide further evidence to support the idea that urbanisation is an integral part of development. Note also that during the second half of the 20th century the highest rates of urbanisation occurred in the LEDCs of the South. For them the level of urbanisation more than doubled whereas in the MEDCs of the North the level increased by slightly less than half.

Figure 1.5 A geographical analysis of urbanisation, 1950–2000

	Urban population as % of total			
	1950	1970	1990	2000 est.
Africa	15.7	22.5	32.8	39.1
South Asia	16.1	21.3	30.6	36.5
East Asia	16.8	26.9	30.0	32.8
Former Soviet Union	39.3	56.7	67.3	70.7
Latin America	41.0	57.4	71.5	76.8
Europe	56.3	66.7	72.8	75.1
Oceania	61.3	70.8	71.1	71.3
North America	63.9	73.8	74.4	74.9
LEDCs	17.0	25.4	33.9	39.3
MEDCs	53.8	66.6	72.5	74.4
World	29.2	37.1	42.9	46.6

SECTION E

The global situation

Figure **1.6** shows the global picture of urbanisation at the national level in the mid-1990s. The following points might be highlighted:

- The lowest levels of urbanisation are in Africa (particularly south of the Sahara) and South-East Asia. In some countries, such as Bhutan, Burundi and Rwanda, the figure remains below 10 per cent.
- The highest levels of urbanisation are dispersed around the globe, in Western Europe, Canada, Argentina and Chile, Australia and New Zealand. It would be wrong to think that such high levels only occur in countries with high population densities; look at the situation in the thinly-populated Middle East. In fact, it is only in Western Europe that high levels of national population density and urbanisation go together.
- Because of the vast extent of Russia, the map conveys the wrong impression that much of the northern part of Asia is quite highly urbanised.

Figure 1.6 Global urbanisation by country, 1995

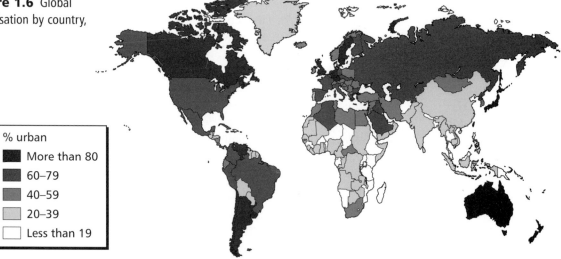

% urban
- More than 80
- 60–79
- 40–59
- 20–39
- Less than 19

An outstanding feature of 20th-century urbanisation was the growth of really large cities with populations numbered in millions. The metropolitan area of Tokyo, for example, now has a population in excess of 25 million; New York's figure is close to 20 million. In the first half of the century, **million cities** were mainly found in the MEDCs. Since 1950, while the

TRINITY GRAMMAR SCHOOL

number of million cities has continued to increase, the majority of them have been in LEDCs – cities such as Bangkok and Jakarta, Addis Ababa and Lagos, Guayaquil and Recife. China now has nearly 40 such cities.

If we take a broad view of global urban history, we might see it as embracing three **urban revolutions** – times of great change. The first revolution took place in prehistoric times and in the so-called 'fertile crescent' of Asia. This led to the first towns and cities. The second and third revolutions are reflected in the shift in the distribution of million cities. The second revolution was part of the Industrial Revolution that swept Western Europe and North America during the 19th century. The growth of mining and manufacturing was not the only change to create urban settlements. A rising demand for centralised services together with developments in transport encouraged the build-up of huge cities and conurbations. The third urban revolution is still under way. It has been sweeping the less developed parts of the world since the middle of the 20th century. It is rather different. It has less to do with industrialisation, and rather more with massive rural–urban migration, high rates of natural increase, and development in general.

Review

15 Summarise the character of each of the three urban revolutions.

SECTION F

Suburbanisation and counterurbanisation

Million cities – indeed all towns – are the outcome of **agglomeration**: the coming together of people and their activities at particular places. Rural–urban migration is an important source of urban growth. So too is natural increase among those people and activities already located in towns and cities (**1.7**). The very act of urban growth soon gives rise to processes operating in an outward direction. Because more has to be accommodated, so the built-up area extends outwards by a process of accretion. This centrifugal tendency has been emphasised during the 20th century by the process of **suburbanisation**. Due to transport developments, people have moved out from the areas of older housing in search of more spacious and modern housing. Shops and social services have followed the outward shift of their customers. Improved transport has allowed people to live at increasing distances from their place of work and from services. Factories as well as labour have moved out of inner-city locations in search of more and cheaper space.

Another key feature of the suburb and suburbanisation is the move to lower building densities. The built-up area has in a sense been opened up. Bricks and mortar are diluted by green space in the form of larger gardens, parks and public sports grounds. As a result of these lower densities, the boundaries between town and country have become even more blurred. The urban edge is now characterised by new landmarks such as large shopping centres, warehouses and distribution centres, office and science parks, golf courses and garden centres.

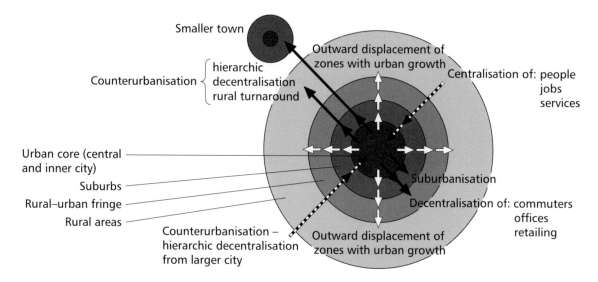

Figure 1.7 Spatial processes associated with urbanisation

The following labels appear in the figure:

- Smaller town
- Counterurbanisation { hierarchic decentralisation, rural turnaround }
- Outward displacement of zones with urban growth
- Centralisation of: people, jobs, services
- Urban core (central and inner city)
- Suburbs
- Rural–urban fringe
- Rural areas
- Suburbanisation
- Decentralisation of: commuters, offices, retailing
- Counterurbanisation – hierarchic decentralisation from larger city
- Outward displacement of zones with urban growth

Today, another decentralisation process is beginning to take hold in more highly-urbanised countries; this is **counterurbanisation** (**1.7**). It is this that leads us to think that there might be a fifth phase on the urbanisation curve (**1.2**). Sadly, the process is widely misunderstood and often confused with suburbanisation. It combines two important strands.

First, there is the fact that some urban people are showing an increasing preference for rural locations. The 'flight from the city' started some time ago with the dispersal of retired people anxious to spend their last years in calmer, cheaper and more attractive locations. They are now followed by growing numbers of commuters, and they in turn by various activities, such as research and development, offices and health clinics. This part of the process has been described as **rural turnaround**.

Secondly, it is the largest cities that have experienced the largest outflows. What is more important, though, is the fact that much of this decentralisation has ended up, not in country locations, but in smaller cities and towns. In other words, some decentralisation has been down the urban hierarchy. We might term this second strand **hierarchic decentralisation**, while the slogan 'small is beautiful' perhaps best gives the flavour of this change.

It is tempting to see counterurbanisation as being anti-urban and as representing the end of urbanisation. True, it is causing the urbanisation curves of some countries to show an increasing downturn (**1.2, 1.3**). But the percentage of a population living in urban settlements is not necessarily the best indicator of the level of urbanisation. Certainly, there is nothing anti-urban in hierarchic decentralisation. Clearly, it is benefiting smaller towns and cities. Equally, it may be that those people and businesses who are part of the rural turnaround and who desert to the countryside are simply helping to spread urbanism beyond the built-up area. In the light of all this, perhaps it would be more appropriate to refer to both strands as **urban deconcentration** (see **Chapter 6**).

Review

16 Explain the difference between **centralisation** and **decentralisation**, and provide urban examples of both.

17 Explain the factors that have made the suburb the major feature of 20th-century urban growth.

18 Debate the issue that counterurbanisation is not an anti-urban process.

TRINITY GRAMMAR SCHOOL

1 From **1.3** select one of the phase 1 countries and find out what factors might be holding back the rate and level of urbanisation.

2 Referring to **1.3**, compare a phase 4 country with a phase 5 country in terms of those factors encouraging high levels of urbanisation.

3 Find out more about the first urban revolution.
   - Where did it occur?
   - Why did it occur?
   Name some of the earliest cities.

4 Write a report about the possible links between development and urbanisation using the data for Sweden and Ethiopia (**1.8**).

Figure 1.8 Statistics for Ethiopia and Sweden

Measure*	Ethiopia	Sweden
Area (1000km²)	1222	57
Urban population 1950 (% total pop.)	5	66
Urban population (% total pop.)	13	83
Total population (millions)	55.5	8.9
Birth rate (per 1000 people)	48	13
Death rate (per 1000 people)	18	12
Infant mortality (per 1000 live births)	122	6
GNP per capita ($)	100	24 830
Manufacturing (% of GDP)	10	31
Services (% of GDP)	29	67
Adult literacy (%)	33	99
Education expenditure (% of GNP)	4.8	6.5
Population per doctor	33 000	395
Human Development Index	0.227	0.929

* Unless stated otherwise, all data relate to 1995

Cities great and small

Size, frequency and rank

This chapter investigates two closely related questions. How do towns and cities grow? Why do urban settlements grow at different rates – in other words, why do some grow into cities and metropolises and others do not? We start by dealing with the second question.

There is plenty of evidence of differential urban growth. If we look at any well-populated area of the Earth's surface, particularly in an MEDC, we notice that its settlement system (i.e. the network of settlements) shows the hierarchic structure mentioned in **Chapter 1 Section B**. The system is made up of a large number of villages, a smaller number that have grown into towns and an even smaller number that have become cities. These frequencies of different settlement sizes have been observed to be quite similar in different areas. When such frequencies are graphed (size plotted against frequency), the distribution often shows up as a smooth, concave curve (**2.1a**). However, if those same frequencies are graphed using logarithmic scales, they produce a straight line. These straight-line relationships are described as being **lognormal**.

Another interesting relationship is shown when settlement size is plotted against rank. **Rank** is the position a particular settlement holds if all the settlements of an area are placed in order of decreasing size. If logarithmic scales are used, then again for many areas the regression will take the form of a straight line (**2.1b**). Such a distribution can be created by a simple formula known as the **rank–size rule**:

$$p_i = P / r_i$$

This states that the size of a particular settlement (p_i) is inversely proportional to its rank (r_i) and the size of the largest city (P). So the second largest city will have a population half that of the largest city. The third largest city's population will be one-third that of the largest, and so on.

Figure 2.1

Lognormal settlement distributions

(a) Frequency–size

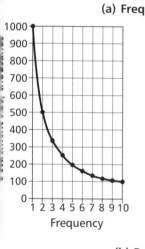

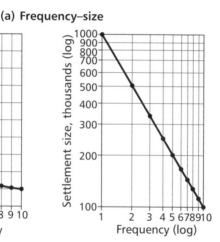

(b) Rank–size

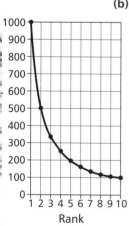

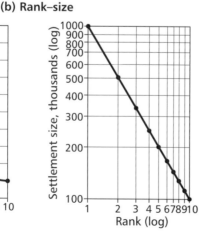

These **lognormal distributions** or straight-line relationships between settlement size and frequency, and between settlement size and rank, are thought to exist in mature and well-balanced settlement systems. Such systems might be expected in most MEDCs with their high levels of urbanisation. However, research into lognormal settlement-size frequencies has shown that the situation is not quite so clear-cut. True, they do occur in some highly-urbanised countries such as Belgium, Germany, Switzerland and the USA. However, they are also found in large countries, such as China, India and South Africa, which have much lower levels of urbanisation.

As for rank–size relationships, it has to be said that lognormality is the exception rather than the rule. In the majority of cases, for example, the largest city is more than twice the size of the second largest, and often by a considerable margin. In these situations, with the largest city standing head and shoulders above the rest of the settlements, the term **primacy** is used. By virtue of being more than five times the size of Guadalajara, Mexico City may claim to be Mexico's **primate** capital city.

It used to be thought that a primate distribution was typical of countries in the early phases of the urbanisation curve (**1.2**). Again, research has taught us to be cautious. LEDCs such as the Dominican Republic, Guatemala, Sri Lanka and Thailand certainly fit the bill, but countries like Denmark, Japan, the Netherlands and Sweden certainly do not. All that may be safely said here is that primate distributions seem to be typical of small countries, particularly those with strong central government and a relatively short urban history.

Figure 2.2 Rank–size distributions for China and Japan

Case study: Rank–size relationships in China and Japan

(a) China

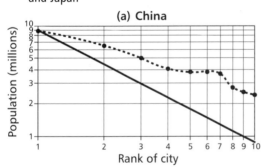

(b) Japan

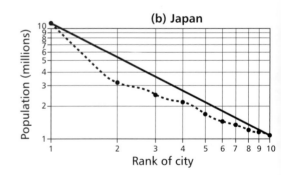

The rank–size distribution for China appears quite straight-lined and therefore fairly lognormal (**2.2a**). However, if the rank–size rule is applied, the population of the 10th city (Dalian) should be 0.893 million, i.e. one-tenth of Shanghai's population of 8.93 million. In fact, it is

2.4 million. Indeed, the actual plot for China consistently pitches at a higher level than the expected plot based on the rank–size rule. A major factor in explaining this deviation must be the immense scale of China's population.

In contrast, the rank–size distribution for Japan pitches below the plot produced by application of the rank–size rule (**2.2b**). More than anything else this reflects the primacy of Tokyo. It is over three times larger than the second city Yokohama (11.93 million compared with 3.29 million).

Whilst Japan is dwarfed by China in terms of its physical extent and population, its mean population density is much higher (332 persons per km^2 compared with 127) and also its level of urbanisation (77 per cent of the population is urban compared with 27 per cent). No doubt it is differences such as these that help to explain the difference in the character of the two rank–size distributions. But maybe there are other factors at work?

Review

1 Try to explain the apparent relationships between:
a lognormality and large countries
b primacy and small countries.

Sources of urban growth

The existence of settlements of different sizes attests to the fact that settlements grow at different rates and to different degrees. To try to explain this differential growth within the settlement system of a country, we need to ask the basic question: what makes settlements grow?

The starting-point of the answer to the question might be that towns grow and prosper because they are well located and accessible. Location and accessibility are significant to urban growth in two ways. They are important to the success of urban economic activities. They are also important when it comes to exerting over surrounding areas the political power that comes with urban economic success.

Towns and cities today are first and foremost economic creatures. Most have come into being to satisfy a wide range of economic needs that can reach across the four sectors. In the **primary sector**, it is likely to be the exploitation of point-bound resources such as minerals and energy. In the **secondary sector**, it will be the processing of localised raw materials and the production of finished goods. In the **tertiary sector**, the provision of commercial and social services is paramount, while in the **quaternary sector** the needs relate to government and administration, decision-making, research and development.

Review

2 Which of the four sectors do you think is likely to provide the greatest source of urban growth? Justify your choice.

Clearly, the fuel of urban growth can involve an almost infinite number of different combinations of economic activity. The actual mix can and does vary from town to town, from country to country, from time to time. For this reason, it becomes difficult to make generalisations about the sources of urban growth and their potency. To help us overcome this difficulty, we might take a quick look at one theory beloved by settlement geographers.

Central-place theory

It is not the intention to go into central-place theory in any detail. The theory has more than its fair share of exposure in many textbooks. The aim here is simply to demonstrate that central-place activity may well be a force behind differential growth within settlement systems. For our purposes, it helps to explain relative success and failure in the evolution of towns and cities.

Central-place theory is based on the fact that virtually all urban settlements provide goods and services for a tributary area. Each good and service has its own particular threshold and range values. **Threshold** is the minimum number of sales that have to be made in order for an activity to remain in business. **Range** is the distance over which a good or service will be marketed. In other words, it is the distance people are prepared to travel in order to acquire the good or service.

The spatial organisation of central-place activity is such that those goods and services with the same threshold and range values will come together. By this process, goods and services with high threshold and range values will create high-order central places. Another outcome is that high-order central places will be located much further apart than low-order central places. As a consequence, they will also be fewer in number.

There is much competition within the central-place system. The winners in the struggle become the high-order central places. Given that there is a broad correlation between central-place status and settlement size, we can begin to understand that status and varying success in the context of central-place activity may well be a force in differential urban growth.

Central-place theory also helps to explain the development of lognormal settlement systems. The volume and distribution of purchasing power within a region or country, while sustaining a large number of low-order central places, are only going to be able to support a limited number of high-order central places.

Figure 2.3 Central-place hierarchy and continuum

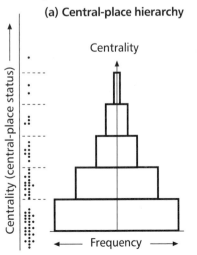

(a) Central-place hierarchy

Centrality

Centrality (central-place status)

← Frequency →

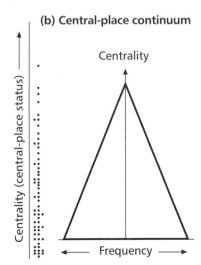

(b) Central-place continuum

Centrality

Centrality (central-place status)

← Frequency →

A crucial aspect of central-place theory is its claim that the central-place network of any area is a class system made up of distinct tiers or orders (**2.3a**). Empirical evidence, however, suggests that the central-place system is not a hierarchy. More often it resembles a **continuum**. In other words, when central places are ranked according to their status, there is a continuous and unbroken sequence from the highest to the lowest status. If we locate all the central places of an area on a **centrality** scale (a measure of the quality and range of services provided), the array of values does not show the clustering of an hierarchic structure (**2.3b**).

Recognition that the central-place system may be a continuum rather than a hierarchy makes life a bit more difficult. The beauty of a hierarchy is that it allows us to generalise about the character and behaviour of all those settlements that fall within a particular class or order. With the continuum, however, each central place is unique. Each occupies a unique niche in the central-place system.

Despite all this, the central-place continuum idea is still relevant to the central task of this chapter. We are still able to argue that there is a strong correlation between central-place ranking and settlement size, and therefore that the spatial organisation of central-place activity helps to explain differential urban growth. Central-place theory also reminds us of another important point. It is that towns and cities derive much of their growth from outside their built-up areas. Every successful town or city needs a hinterland or tributary area – the larger the better. That tributary area may supply a range of things from raw materials for manufacturing to a market for processed goods, from labour to fill a wide range of urban jobs to customers for commercial and social services.

Figure 2.4 The higher orders of central place in England and Wales

Case study: The central-place hierarchy of England and Wales

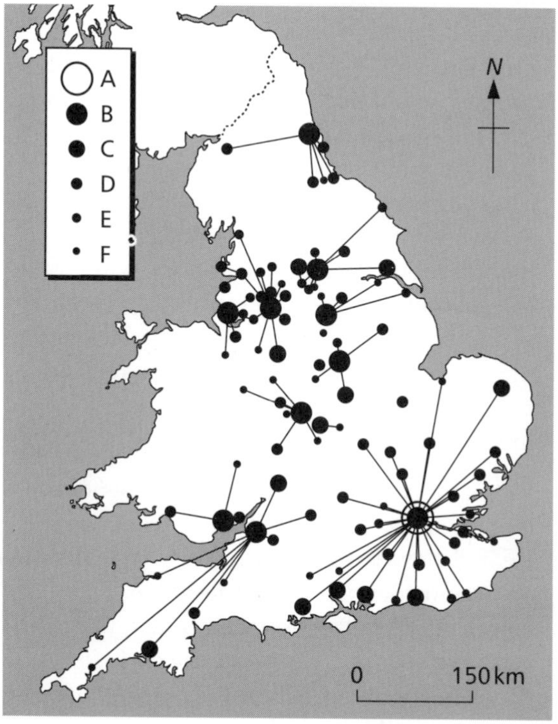

Empirical studies have recognised distinct orders of central place in England and Wales. However, the number of orders varies from study to study and according to the measures used to assess centrality. Figure **2.4** shows one such scheme in which six different orders are recognised in the upper ranks of the central-place hierarchy.

At the top of the hierarchy there is London which is in a class of its own. All other central places are deemed to be subservient to it. London has a tributary area that is truly nationwide. Below London are the B central places, the regional capitals like Birmingham, Manchester, Bristol and Cardiff. Figure **2.4** indicates that all the lower orders of central place (C, D, E and F) are organised into sub-systems, each being dependent on a regional capital. It is important to note that London also functions at this level.

As we move down the central-place hierarchy, it is possible to recognise at each order another series of sub-systems. For example, D, E and F central places 'nest' in the sub-systems commanded by C centres; E and F central places are involved in the sub-systems of D central places; and so on down the hierarchy. What this map does not show are the lower orders of central place. In this instance, they probably range from what we would call modest market towns right down to small rural settlements with their one remaining shop.

In summary, the central-place hierarchy of England and Wales is a complex but well-integrated system made up of interlocking and overlapping spheres of influence. It has a cellular structure. Apart from London and the lowest rank of central place, all central places are integrated into the overall system in two ways:

- by being subservient to a higher order of central place
- by commanding their own sub-systems of lower-order central places.

Review

3 Count the number of central places in each of the six orders shown in **2.4**. Does your arithmetic evidence support the idea that there is a central-place hierarchy?

4 Can you think of anything that might upset the generalisation that the larger the urban settlement, the higher its central-place status?

The metropolitan explosion

Figure 2.5 Factors encouraging large-scale urban agglomeration

Perhaps the most striking evidence today of differential urban growth are the huge metropolitan areas around the world. They have populations measured in millions. During the first half of the 20th century, such areas were confined to MEDCs. Examples would have been London, New York and Paris. Since then, they have emerged in LEDCs, as in India (Bombay, Calcutta and Delhi), China (Beijing and Shanghai) and Brazil (Rio de Janeiro and São Paulo). Whatever their location, these metropolitan areas are clearly the winners in the competitive struggle for urban supremacy at a national, if not an international level. So how is their success to be explained? The answer lies in unravelling a number of interrelated factors (**2.5**).

Communication economies
- efficient personal contact
- low transport cost

Cumulative causation
- first in the field
- multiplier effects

URBAN AGGLOMERATION

Status-symbol syndrome
- prestige of being at the centre of things

Mass-gravity effect
- scale economies
- success breeds success

We might start by pointing out the benefits that businesses of all sorts reap from being located close to linked enterprises (**localisation** or **communication economies**)(**2.5**). This allows effective face-to-face contact; transport costs are reduced. Convergence and concentration are encouraged, as they are also by the fact that businesses are able to share rather than bear alone the costs of such things as public utilities, transport infrastructure and specialist services (**agglomeration economies**). Adding to the momentum of these economies is the **mass-gravity effect** whereby size attracts size.

It is not just by chance that a large proportion of metropolitan areas are state or national capitals. Being near to the ministries and elected **decision-makers** of government is a strong attraction, particularly to the decision-makers in the private sector. Thus companies are attracted to locate their headquarters close to the seat of government and this, in turn, attracts many linked or related businesses. Supporting this is the fact that most metropolitan economies show quite well-developed **quaternary sectors**.

Chance is, however, a significant element in the next strand of explanation. The argument goes that each metropolitan area had its origins in some initial advantage. Once that advantage was seized, the process of **cumulative causation** and its **multiplier effects** set in (**2.5**). These forces strengthen and make more competitive the particular city as compared with later-comers to the scene. So here the idea is that the 'first in the queue' is the one most likely to succeed. Compared with other cities in their national urban systems, most metropolitan areas have a long history and indeed were amongst the first urban settlements.

Finally, we need to return to the point that metropolitan areas are frequently capital cities. The capital city has a certain ethos. People perceive it to command some sort of special status. It becomes a desirable and prestigious place in which to live and work. This perception draws in large numbers of people. The attraction is rather more than just higher wages, better jobs and services or nearness to the seat of government. It has a psychological dimension. We might call this the **status-symbol syndrome**.

Case study: Metropolitan contrasts – Cairo and London

	Cairo	London
Population, 1995 (millions)	6.8	7.0
Annual growth rate, 1975–85 (%)	2.4	–1.1
Annual growth rate, 1985–95 (%)	2.3	–0.5
Extent of built-up area (ha)	214	1578
Population density, 1995 (persons/km^2)	31 775	4436
Smoke concentrations, 1990 (SPM)	49	32
Road traffic (traffic flow at rush hour/mph)	12.4	10.4
Housing (% dwellings with piped water)	94.0	100.0

Figure 2.6 Basic statistics relating to Cairo and London

The statistics in **2.6** tell a tale of two very different cities and scenarios. London, like so many leading cities in MEDCs, actually lost population during the second half of the 20th century, principally because of decentralisation and net out-migration. London was at its most dynamic during the late 19th and early 20th centuries. In contrast, Cairo epitomises many of the leading cities of LEDCs. Fast growth has resulted from a rising volume of net in-migration and high rates of natural increase.

Review

5 Can you think of any other reasons why a town succeeds in eventually becoming a metropolis?

6 Write a brief account summarising the metropolitan differences shown in **2.6**.

SECTION E

Megalopolis

During the second half of the 20th century a further scaling-up of urban growth took place. Modern transport developments encouraged metropolitan areas, conurbations and cities to coalesce into an even higher order of urban settlement termed **megalopolis**. The megalopolitan phenomenon was first noted along the eastern seaboard of the USA. Stretching from Boston to Washington DC, it embraces New York, Philadelphia and Baltimore. Since then a similar structure has emerged in California running from San Francisco to Los Angeles. On the other side of the Pacific, there is Japan's megalopolitan corridor running along the southern coastlands of Honshu (**2.7**). In the UK, the building of Milton Keynes has filled in the urban break between Greater London and Greater Birmingham and so we now have a megalopolis extending from London to Manchester and Merseyside. In France, a megalopolitan structure is emerging in the Lower Rhône Valley from Lyons down to Marseilles. On the other side of the world, a similar structure is beginning to be defined linking Sydney and Melbourne.

Let us gain some impression of the scale of megalopolis. Something like 20 per cent of the American population lives in 'Bowash' megalopolis along the eastern seaboard complex. Half the Japanese population lives in Tokaido megalopolis, and a similar proportion of the British people live in the so-called 'axial belt'. Clearly, there are economies and benefits to be derived from having so much of a nation's human resources so concentrated. Presumably, the same factors apply as in the case of metropolitan areas. But no doubt there may be others. Equally, there must be serious costs. Not least of these is the effect that the growth of megalopolis might have on the rest of the country.

Case study: Tokaido megalopolis

Tokaido megalopolis is located along the Pacific coast of Japan's main island, Honshu (**2.7**). It stretches from the capital Tokyo to the port city of Kobe. Located within this coastal belt are seven of Japan's eleven 'million' cities. These, in their turn, are incorporated into three metropolitan regions which centre on Tokyo, Nagoya and Osaka. During the second half of the 20th century, ribbons of urban development grew along the major

Figure 2.7 The structure of Tokaido megalopolis

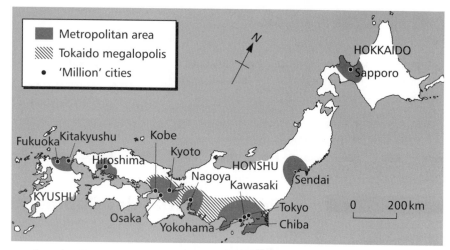

road and rail routes linking these metropolitan areas. As a consequence, they gradually became welded together to form a single megalopolitan structure.

A considerable proportion of Japan's economy and population is concentrated in Tokaido megalopolis. While the megalopolis accounts for a little less than 20 per cent of Japan's land area, it contains 55 per cent of its population and just over 60 per cent of its GDP.

West of Kobe, there are three more 'million' cities: Hiroshima, Fukuoka and Kitakyushu. The last two are in fact located on the southern island of Kyushu. Given their relatively nearness to each other and the good transport infrastructure that now links them, it seems highly likely that the megalopolitan structure will soon extend westwards beyond Kobe. The enlarged megalopolis will account for an even greater share of Japan's population and economic wealth. Is it a good thing to have so much of a nation's assets concentrated in what is effectively a single urban complex and a relatively small part of its territory? Think of the degree to which it drains resources from other parts of Japan.

It is clear from the last two sections that 20th-century urbanisation has produced some huge urban settlements – so vast that they can even be observed from space. The metropolitan and megalopolitan areas are clearly the super-champions of the urban growth league. In explaining their emergence, there is a strong feeling that success breeds success. Successful growth lies rooted in the command of a sizeable tributary area. In the case of metropolitan areas, the hinterland most often is on an international scale. The term **global city** seems an appropriate one (see **Chapters 3** and **7**). But the final word here must be one of caution. With the onset of **counterurbanisation** in some of the more highly-urbanised countries, it looks as if it is the largest urban settlements that are the first in the firing line. **Urban deconcentration** (decentralisation) appears to be starting at the top of the urban hierarchy and hitting the most successful first. However, the outlook for the largest cities is far from gloomy, for reasons that are outlined in the next section.

7 Make two lists, one showing what you believe to be the benefits of megalopolis, the other its costs. Which list do you think is the more significant?

8 Rural–urban migration is one factor in the evolution of megalopolis. Identify others.

9 What factors might discourage the westward extension of Tokaido megalopolis?

10 Suggest reasons why urban decentralisation in MEDCs seems to start in the largest cities.

SECTION F

Post-industrial developments

De-industrialisation

The rise of many cities in Europe and North America was associated with the growth of industry. Manufacturing goods provided a potent fuel for urban development. This was particularly the case during the 19th and early 20th centuries. However, all that started to change in the 1970s with the onset of **de-industrialisation**. The manufacturing sector began to decline and high levels of unemployment came to plague older industrial cities. De-industrialisation seems to have prompted three significant processes.

- **Factory closures** These have been particularly marked in the inner areas of the British conurbations like Clydeside, Merseyside, Manchester, the West Midlands and West Yorkshire. Factory closures started in the 1950s with the decentralisation of businesses to the suburbs and beyond. In the 1960s and 1970s, factory closures accelerated as more and more companies went into liquidation. Bankruptcy was largely brought about by keen competition from overseas factories, by failing to invest in new and more efficient production methods and by restrictive government policies keen to squeeze polluting industries out of the inner city. In the 1980s some attempt was made to reduce the rate of industrial decline. The creation of Enterprise Zones and Urban Development Corporations (see **Chapter 3 Section B**) and the building of science and industrial parks are examples of the wish to revive the industrial fortunes of the inner city. They have done little to ease levels of unemployment.

- **Migration of jobs to the suburbs and beyond** It is hardly surprising that factories should be tempted to either set up in or move to the suburbs and beyond. Above all, these new locations offer cheaper and more extensive sites with good accessibility in terms of the motorway network. These locations provide manufacturers with the opportunity to leave behind inner-city congestion and outdated factories. They can start afresh with spacious buildings capable of housing modern assembly-line production. Given the parallel shift of people to the suburbs and dormitory settlements, recruiting labour is scarcely a problem. Indeed, with journey-to-work distances cut and with a more flexible management of labour, there has been a gender shift in the labour force. The suburban factories employ a high proportion of women.

- **Migration of jobs overseas** It is quite clear that many industrial jobs in MEDCs have been lost to newly-industrialised countries and other countries well down the development league table. The **transnational corporations** have played an important part in this **global decentralisation**. The availability of cheap, unskilled and non-unionised labour has been the key location factor.

The urban significance of de-industrialisation seems to be as follows:

- its impact has been greatest on the large cities of Europe and North America
- it has encouraged a decline in the populations of those cities
- its social impact has been most marked on the less mobile social groups still trapped in the inner city
- an 'economic vacuum' has been created in inner city areas.

The service economy

During the 1980s and into the 1990s there was a marked rise in service sector jobs. This was prompted by:

- a growth in corporate headquarters – a need for more people to co-ordinate the spatially dispersed activities of large companies
- a rising demand in the business community for producer services such as specialist financial and legal services, advertising and management consultancy
- an expanding consumer demand for services related to leisure and quality of life
- a growth in research and development.

The employment created by this growth in the service sector has been somewhat polarised between managerial posts and 'back office' jobs. The former have been few in number. The latter are typically routine, low-paid, low-skilled and temporary or part-time. As such, they have failed to provide suitable jobs for the semi-skilled and formerly well-paid workers made redundant by de-industrialisation. Indeed, the total growth of jobs in the UK's service sector since the end of the Second World War has failed to completely compensate the loss of manufacturing jobs. Thus unemployment remains a problem in most MEDC towns and cities.

The location of these new services also seems to be polarised. Corporate headquarters have always favoured central-city locations. The large transnational corporations continue to concentrate in the very largest cities, the truly **global cities** like New York, London and Tokyo. They need access to national and international markets, specialist services and a pool of highly skilled and educated labour. Since the customers of producer services are the headquarters of transnational corporations, they too have become concentrated in the central areas of global cities.

The consumer services show an altogether more dispersed location. They are quite well distributed through the urban hierarchy rather than polarised in the top-tier cities. Their location is increasingly suburban and on the edge of town rather than in the central city. Nearness to the affluent populations of the suburbs is a key location factor. The location of research and development facilities (R & D) is determined by three needs: to be near to company headquarters, to production units and to highly-qualified labour. These requirements tend to be partially satisfied in one of four locations:

- in large cities with corporate headquarters
- in modern industrial estates and business parks
- in cities with universities and other types of research institution
- in attractive residential environments (to attract suitable labour).

Summing up

Globalisation in the post-industrial era is creating higher levels of interdependence. Interdependence is increasing between countries and between a small number of cities making up an elite league of primate global cities. These cities are the seats of those transnational corporations that direct so much of the global economy. They attract the most recent advances in **telecommunications** (fax, e-mail, computer networks, the Internet and virtual reality). As a result, they are being drawn closer together by expanding and almost instantaneous flows of information. The decision-making that goes on in them is instantly transmitted to all parts of the global economy.

Moving down the urban hierarchy, however, the concentration of advanced communication technologies falls off, as does connectivity with the world economy. Older industrial cities, the cities of LEDCs and rural areas are finding themselves increasingly distanced from the centres of the global economy. So what seems to be emerging is a geographical pattern of two parts. The first comprises a small number of 'information-rich' global cities involved in an intensively interconnected transnational urban network. The second part is made up of the 'information-poor' hinterlands immediately surrounding these global cities and with which they are poorly connected. That is the face of differential growth today.

Review

11 Explain what is meant by **de-industrialisation** and **globalisation**.

12 Suggest reasons for the growth of the **service economy**.

13 Explain what is meant by the statement: 'Some locations are moving closer together.'

1 a For each of the four countries in **2.8**, plot on logarithmic graph paper (i) the data and (ii) the expected distribution based on the rank–size rule as applied to that data.

 b Write an analytical account which compares (i) the two plots for each country and (ii) the actual rank–size relationships of the four countries.

For each of the next two enquiries, refer to library sources and relevant information taken off the Internet.

2 Write a reasoned explanation for each of the following:

 a London's accelerating growth during the 19th century.

 b The growing tide of decentralisation from London since 1950.

 c The rising volume of migration into Cairo.

3 Compare Cairo and London in terms of:

 a their sites

 b their economic bases

 c their spatial patterns of land use

 d their social patterns.

Rank	Brazil		Egypt		Indonesia		Italy	
1	São Paulo	9480	Cairo	6800	Jakarta	8259	Rome	2723
2	Rio de Janeiro	5336	Alexandria	3380	Surabaya	2421	Milan	1359
3	Salvador	2056	El Giza	2144	Bandung	2027	Naples	1072
4	Belo Horizonte	2049	Shubra el Kheim	834	Medan	1686	Turin	923
5	Forteleza	1758	Port Said	460	Palembang	1084	Palermo	697
6	Brasilia	1596	El Mahalla	408	Semarang	1005	Genoa	668
7	Curitiba	1290	Suez	388	Ujung Pandang	913	Bologna	401
8	Recife	1290	Tanta	380	Malang	650	Florence	397
9	Nova Iguaçu	1286	El Mansura	371	Surakarta	504	Bari	342
10	Port Alegre	1263	Helwan	328	Padang	477	Catania	330

Figure 2.8 Rank–size data for a sample of four countries (populations (1995) in thousands)

The coming of the post-industrial city

The developments discussed in the last section of the previous chapter, together with the process of decentralisation, are beginning to have an impact on traditional urban form. Urban geographers refer increasingly to the emergence of a **post-industrial** or **post-modern city**. Its form is diverging from the structure described in the concentric zone, sector and multiple nuclei models. These models were based on the so-called **industrial** or **modern city** of MEDCs in the first half of the 20th century. A feature highlighted by all those models was the tendency for similar activities and similar people to agglomerate. This, in turn, led to the creation of homogenous areas within the built-up area, each distinguished by the presence of a dominant land use or social group. The spatial arrangement of these areas was strongly conditioned by the general decline in land values outwards from the city centre.

Since this spatial sorting of land use is well covered in most A-level Geography textbooks (e.g. *Environment and People*, Chapter 33.3), little is to be gained from going over the ground yet again. Rather the discussion should move on to examine the processes that are beginning to change familiar patterns. Those changes are outlined here and revisited in greater detail in **Chapter 4**.

Changing character

One of the features of the post-industrial city is its much more fragmented pattern. The term **urban mosaic** perhaps best describes the emerging new form. It conveys the image of something made up of many very small parts. We might also imagine that the pictorial pattern of the mosaic is a fairly loose and uniform one. It does not have a dominant central motif. This reflects another important feature of the post-industrial city, namely a loss of focus and overall coherence. In the post-industrial city, the CBD has lost some of its dominance. It is now rivalled by prestige developments that pepper the urban landscape rather like sporadic rock outcrops. These new nodes of investment are separated by tracts of old urban fabric which are degrading economically, socially and environmentally.

Hall (1998) has provided a useful summary of the features that distinguish the modern and post-industrial cities (**3.1**).

A postscript is needed here to make the point that not all cities in the North fall into one of these two categories. Indeed, it is appropriate to

	Modern	**Post-industrial**
Urban structure	Homogenous functional and social zones; dominant CBD; declining gradient of land value	Chaotic multi-nodal structure; prestige and spectacular centres; large areas of poverty; high-tech corridors; post-suburban developments
Economy	Industrial – mass production; economies of scale; production-based	Service-sector based; flexible production aimed at niche markets; economies of scope; globalised; telecommunications based; consumption oriented; jobs in newly-developed peripheral zones
Urban government	Managerial – redistribution of resources for social purposes; public provision of essential services	Entrepreneurial – use of resources to attract mobile international capital and investment
Planning	Cities planned as totalities; space shaped for social ends	Spatial 'fragments' designed for aesthetic rather than social ends
Architecture	Functional; mass production of styles	Mix of styles; spectacular; use of heritage
Society	Class divisions; large degree of homogeneity within social / ethnic groups	Highly fragmented, life-style divisions; high degree of social polarisation; groups distinguished by their consumption patterns

Figure 3.1 A comparison of the essential features of modern and post-industrial cities

identify at least a third type, namely the **pre-industrial city**. This would include historic cities such as Bath and York which have retained much of their early urban layout and fabric. They have not completely escaped the impact of modern and post-industrial developments. They have been lightly touched rather than heavily scarred. Equally, it is possible that the character of cities in the South warrants them being recognised as a separate category (see **Section C**). Finally, it needs to be stressed that to date it is only the leading cities of the North that show extensive evidence of a post-industrial transformation. Is it because they are all important control and command points in the global economy?

Review

1 Study **3.1** and in your own words compare modern and post-industrial cities in terms of:
   • economy
   • society
   • structure.

2 For a city that you know at first hand, identify evidence of post-industrial change.

3 Why do you think global cities like London, Los Angeles and Tokyo show the strongest evidence of post-industrial urbanisation?

Who manages the city?

This deceptively simple question is extremely difficult to answer, but it is a question that should be asked if we have any concern about our present towns and cities and the urban future in general. The answer we reach very much depends on the country concerned, particularly the nature of its economy. Table **3.2** shows a possible classification of the major types of economy found in today's world. The following discussion will focus on the mixed economies of the First World, which includes countries such as France, Germany and Japan.

Figure 3.2 A classification of economy types

Global division	Type of economy	Example
First World	Private market	USA
	Mixed economy	UK
Second World	Centrally-planned	China
	Transitional	Hungary
Third World	Private market	Brazil
	Centrally-planned	Tanzania
	Transitional	Vietnam

Diagram **3.3** indicates that there are four main players involved in making the sorts of decision that strongly influence the growth and changing structure of a city. Below we take a look at the role of four of these players, but do not forget the two other players, the employers and service providers.

Figure 3.3 Urban managers and some of their responsibilities

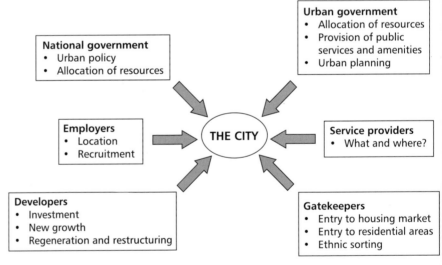

National government
• Urban policy
• Allocation of resources

Urban government
• Allocation of resources
• Provision of public services and amenities
• Urban planning

Employers
• Location
• Recruitment

THE CITY

Service providers
• What and where?

Developers
• Investment
• New growth
• Regeneration and restructuring

Gatekeepers
• Entry to housing market
• Entry to residential areas
• Ethnic sorting

Urban government

There is not a town or city in the world that does not have some form of local government (**3.3**). But the powers and spheres of activity of government at that level cover a huge range. In mixed economies, urban government is responsible for the following areas:

- The general running of the town or city. This is likely to include providing a range of social services, managing the transport systems, supplying public housing for rent, ensuring a proper infrastructure of public services, improving the urban environment, and encouraging new investment in jobs, services and housing.
- The regulation and design of additions to the built-up area. This would cover such responsibilities as reducing the environmental impacts of urban growth, ensuring the proper location of commercial and social services, providing the necessary physical infrastructure, and controlling the mix of housing types to fit the character of local demand.

Most of the second group of responsibilities and some of the first fall within the remit of what we might loosely call **planning**. The precise character of planning at any time depends very much on the political leanings of both local and national governments. In general, it might be said that the more 'left' the government, the greater the planning intervention and the more social its objectives.

One of the important changes involved in the post-industrial city has been the shift away from a strongly regulating type of planning. The planning of the **modern city** was concerned with maintaining the city as an entity and seeing it in its wider context as a central place and employment node. It had strong social aims such as providing good social services and rented housing. It tried in a variety of ways to improve the lot of the urban poor and the most blighted parts of the built-up area. In the **post-industrial city**, the influence of planning over market forces has weakened. Its character has also changed. Instead of regulating, it has become **facilitating**. In other words, planning now seeks to encourage others, mainly developers, to undertake what is needed to improve and extend the urban environment. This is well illustrated by the Urban Development Corporations that were set up in the UK in the 1980s.

Case study: Urban Development Corporations

The Urban Development Corporation (UDC) programme was launched in 1981 and has since become the main government scheme for bringing about urban regeneration. The UDCs aim to encourage the private sector back into run-down inner-city areas. They follow a market-oriented and property-led approach. There are now 12 Corporations (**3.4**).

The responsibilities of the UDCs are wide-ranging. They include:

- the reclamation of derelict land
- the provision of transport infrastructure
- environmental enhancement
- the provision of financial incentives to private-sector developers and non-government organisations.

Figure 3.4
Urban Development Corporations in the UK

	Area (ha)	Population	Employment	Grant aid up to 1992 (£m)
Birmingham Heartland	1000	12 500	n.d.	n.d.
Black Country	2598	35 405	53 000	96
Bristol	420	1000	19 500	22
Cardiff Bay	1093	500	15 000	94
Central Manchester	187	500	15 300	41
Leeds	540	800	n.d.	30
London Docklands	2150	40 400	27 213	813
Merseyside	350	450	1500	72
Sheffield	900	300	18 000	42
Teesside	4858	400	n.d.	110
Trafford Park	1267	40	24 468	76
Tyne & Wear	2375	4500	40 115	110
TOTAL	17 738	96 795	214 596	1506

Each corporation is given a specified shelf-life, usually between 5 and 15 years. After this time has expired, the economic momentum that has been given to the area is expected to sustain further regeneration.

The record of achievement to date suggests that the UDCs:

■ have encouraged a limited amount of private inward investment
■ have attracted property speculation
■ have not done well in terms of creating new jobs
■ have achieved little by way of re-industrialisation.

One aspect of the UDCs that appears to be heavily criticised is the fact that they lie outside the control of the local government authority. Instead they are run by non-elected boards that are accountable only to the government. Some local people voice their fears about this lack of local democratic accountability. They suspect that the real beneficiaries of any regeneration are incoming groups of wealthy people.

See **Case study, Chapter 4 Section B.**

National government

Whether it is labelled as such or not, most governments in the North have a national urban policy (**3.3**). In the mixed economy, government reacts to market forces and at the same time tries to direct those forces through its guidance of public investment. The Urban Development Corporations are one good example; the British New Towns programme of the post-war period is another (see the following **Case study**). The prime aim of the latter was to reduce differences in regional economic growth rates and to stimulate private investment and new economic growth in areas outside London. Running alongside this programme was the government attempt to curb the growth of London and other major conurbations (see **Chapter 6 Sections C and D**).

Inevitably, the urban management undertaken by national governments in mixed economies tends to be broadly based and applied to the urban hierarchy as a whole rather than to specific cities. Even in London's case, the aim of the government was simply to reduce its primacy within the British urban system.

Case study: Planned overspill in Great Britain

Two different overspill devices were used in the early post-war period to curb the growth of Britain's conurbations: the **new town** and the **expanded town**. Both were designed by the government to act as reception centres for people and jobs persuaded to decentralise from the conurbations.

Following the New Towns Act (1946), some 28 new towns were built in Britain, but not all for overspill purposes. The first-generation schemes were launched in the late 1940s and comprised a ring of eight located around London. New towns were also built to meet the needs of the West Midlands, Manchester, Merseyside and Clydeside conurbations. During the 1960s, two important trends in the development of British new towns emerged:

- a move to much larger schemes with population targets set at between 150 000 and 250 000 rather than around 80 000, as was the case with the first-generation new towns
- the expansion of sizeable existing towns like Northampton and Peterborough as new towns.

Milton Keynes, with a population of around 165 000, is probably one of the most successful of Britain's second-generation new towns. No new schemes have been designated since the 1970s.

The second overspill device involved the enlargement of existing towns. In England and Wales the device was launched by the Town Development Act (1952). One of the earliest schemes was the expansion of Swindon. It was initiated in 1954 when its population was 69 000; it now stands at over 150 000. Other notable schemes include Basingstoke and Aylesbury.

It would seem that the second-generation new towns represented a fusion of the two overspill devices. The overall programme appears to have been successful in that all British conurbations have since slimmed down. But was this really due to government intervention, or were there other factors at work?

In centrally-planned economies, the state has much more clout. It both runs the economy and guides investment. In the former Soviet Union, a policy was pursued of spreading urban development as evenly as possible across the country. Attempts were made to limit the size and growth of the largest cities. Because the state was so all-powerful, considerable progress was made in achieving these objectives.

Case study: The socialist city

Although the communist regimes of the Soviet Union and Eastern Europe have collapsed, they have left a legacy in the urban landscape. The socialist city was to be a classless city. This meant that everyone should live in the same type of housing area and the same type of apartment block. In practice this resulted in standardised housing in uniform rows of dreary-looking blocks of poor design and construction (**3.5**). The only exception were the areas of better-quality housing and well-tended lawns where the Communist Party officials lived.

Figure 3.5 A socialist city housing area

Residential areas were organised into small units known as 'micro-neighbourhoods'. Each of these might contain about 15 000 people, shops, a school, a post office and a small park. All services were within a radius of one kilometre. Three or four of these units clustered to form a residential district. Higher-order shopping, cultural and recreational facilities were available in the district centre. This centre was no more than 2km from the furthest dwelling. However, the policy of encouraging pedestrian transport came unstuck when people needed to commute. Frequently the location of major areas of employment required quite long journeys across the city. These could only be undertaken by public transport.

The city centre was rather different from its Western counterpart. In place of commerce and offices, there were buildings housing political, cultural and educational activities. These prestige buildings were located around or near a large central square. The creation of the central square often required the clearance of historic buildings. The square was frequently used for military parades and mass demonstrations in support of the socialist regime. Almost invariably it contained mammoth pieces of heroic socialist sculpture.

Few socialist cities were built from scratch. Most involved remodelling existing towns and cities. Conversion was not always easy. For this reason, the best expressions of the socialist ideal are to be found in the more recently-built suburbs.

Developers

The term **developer** is used to cover all those who invest in the urban area in some way or another (**3.3**). They may be individuals, but more often they are private firms and non-government organisations. They are very much in the business of recycling and extending the built-up area. The whole urban development industry has undergone a major change in the last 15 years or so. It has become more concentrated into a smaller number of very large firms. Smaller firms have either been eliminated or taken over by larger firms; quite sizeable firms have also merged. The consequence for the urban area is that these larger firms are able to undertake projects on a larger scale than was previously the case. Typical of these are the Docklands scheme in London, California Plaza in Los Angeles and the World Financial Centre in New York. These 'mega-projects' show recurring features:

- they involve the recycling of rundown sites
- they are located near to the centres of global cities
- their development is bound up with the workings of the global economy
- they are undertaken by large multinational developers
- they rely on heavy borrowing from banks and other financial institutions.

Case study: La Défense, Paris

La Défense is a mixed-use development comprising an exhibition hall, cinemas, gardens, a shopping centre, restaurants, housing, a large public open space, conference halls and offices. It forms an extension to one of the world's most famous streets and historic urban axes – the Louvre–Champs Elysées axis. Creating it has involved restructuring a substantial tract of the central area of Paris.

The concept behind this flagship development was that it should carry on the French tradition of innovative architecture, design and building technology. It is the outcome of a successful partnership between public and private enterprise.

La Place de la Défense is of such a length that it requires two métro stops, one at each end, to service the development. At ground level, the development appears to consist of huge, perfectly-formed geometric constructions, randomly distributed over a vast paved plane. The large blocks accommodate either offices or apartments with little mixed use within buildings. Beneath the public square is the largest shopping complex in Paris, along with restaurants and cinemas.

Figure 3.6 La Grande Arche, La Défense

Undoubtedly the most striking building in La Défense is La Grande Arche. It is meant to counterbalance the Arc de Triomphe, so that together these two structures mark the ends of an impressive urban axis in post-modern Paris. Within its cubic arch structure, the building (completed in 1989) provides an enormous amount of prestigious office accommodation. Publicity claims La Grande Arche to be 'a symbol and an image of modernity and also of freedom, and an opening towards the future'. The claim might sound outrageous, but it is not too far short of the truth. The building certainly plays its part in making La Défense one of the most impressive flagship developments of the late 20th century.

Although flagship developments reflect well on the huge corporations behind them, there are other developers around of more modest proportions. They are still playing a vital part in the evolution of the urban area. Their activities are diverse and include constructing:

- shopping malls in redeveloped parts of city centres
- new edge-of-town and out-of-town retailing complexes
- prestigious housing projects in up-and-coming inner-city areas
- new suburban housing estates
- high-rise office blocks
- sports centres and suburban golf courses.

Gatekeepers

Gatekeepers are professional people (estate agents, bankers, building society managers, council housing officers) who are influential in the allocation of housing among competing people (**3.3**). Since for most people buying a house requires obtaining credit (a loan or a mortgage) from a bank or building society, the branch managers of these institutions are put in a position of power. In effect they control the 'gate' to home-ownership, closing it to those who are deemed to be a risk or have a poor credit rating. As a consequence, gatekeepers can become quite influential in the spatial sorting of people and ethnic groups within towns and cities. In the USA, for example, estate agents have used their power to direct Black buyers to particular residential areas and away from others.

Outside the owner-occupier housing sector, there are at least two other notable gatekeepers. In the privately rented sector, there are the landlords. In the public sector of council housing, the influential players are the local authority housing officers. In the allocation of housing, the latter have considerable power to determine who goes where. They are also able to deal with the problem of anti-social households either by concentrating them on particular estates or completely debarring their access to public housing.

Summing up

Management of the city involves an unwritten co-operation between players in both the public and private sectors. Their relative influence varies over time depending on the political complexions of changing governments and on the ups and downs of the economic climate. In the era of the post-industrial city, the private sector was riding high during the investment boom of the 1980s. However, with the collapse of the property market in the early 1990s, the public sector has had to raise its profile. Clearly, these shifts in the city's managerial balance do have an impact on urban form and character.

Review

4 What are your thoughts about the question posed towards the end of the 'overspill' case study on page 33?

5 Why do you think the British government was so keen to prevent the conurbations from growing any further?

6 Apart from their prestige, identify possible longer-term benefits of flagship projects.

7 Add to 3.3 by identifying other appropriate responsibilities that each of the six urban managers might exercise.

8 In your own words, explain what is meant in urban geography by a **gatekeeper**.

9 Who are the **service providers (3.3)**?

A view from the South

In the poorer countries of the South, the same set of managers can be identified, but the balance of power is rather different. For example, the ability of national governments to manage cities is limited by their general lack of financial resources. They may have the power to intervene and to determine national urban policy, but they most often lack what it takes to implement such policy. In the event, the economy and investment are often controlled by **foreign enterprises** – an additional breed of urban manager. Vital decisions about what goes on in the larger cities are made in boardrooms in London, New York and Tokyo. Lack of finance and the persistence of external control mean that national urban policy is limited in scope.

Relative to their counterparts in the North, city authorities suffer the same drawbacks as their national governments: a lack of resources and a lack of control. Many may have some sort of master plan or vision, but any implementation is at the mercy of developers. Indeed, developers are typically the key players. Because they are hardly constrained by rules and regulations, they are free almost to do as they wish. Gatekeepers exist, but they are not the same. Rather than bank and building society managers, it is the **wealthy** who exercise their power and influence. It is they who keep watch over the areas of high-class housing and attractive sites for future development.

In the cities of the South we may recognise another two additional players in urban decision-making. First, there are those involved in both official and non-government aid programmes. **Aid officials** can have quite a say, as for example in deciding which slum or shanty areas might be helped to upgrade or where a new school or medical centre will be located. Secondly, there are those millions of **individuals** who make their own decisions and who collectively make their mark on the city. What are the shanty towns and squatter settlements other than the outcome of people deciding that this is where they are going to live? And this is where they will stay until they either manage to break out of the cycle of poverty or are forcibly moved on.

Case study: Encouraging news from Guatemala City

In 1986, a newly-elected government established a committee charged with improving basic services in Guatemala City. Committee members included representatives from:

- several government ministries
- the City authorities
- local universities
- non-government organisations
- international aid agencies (e.g. the World Bank, UNICEF)
- local low-income community groups.

Partnership has been the key word, involving the pooling of resources, experience, expertise and hopes. Action has been taken, in parallel, along four related fronts.

The provision of a network of health promoters and pharmacies. By 1993, 600 community health promoters were active in 60 illegal or informal settlements and were serving over 150 000 inhabitants (this in a city of 2 million). Their task is to monitor the general health of neighbourhoods and to see that appropriate action is taken if an outbreak of disease threatens.

Improvement of water supply. The single-source tank idea has proved quite effective. A single large water tank, connected to the urban supply network, is installed in a neighbourhood by the City authorities. From this source the local community create their own supply network to reach individual dwellings. UNICEF provided the funds for the pipes and other materials. Each family carried out the work to make their own home connection. Water supply is metered and the local community collects fees from residents and pays the city's water company.

Improvement of housing. Loans have been provided to residents at a monthly cost that low-income households can afford. The resident selects one of five approved house designs and then, using the loan, builds a new dwelling. The designs allow for the construction of a second storey in later years. Loans are also available for families to upgrade their homes. Schemes also include the installation of drains and sewers, paving streets and building community centres.

Introduction of day-care for young children. Experience had shown that pre-school children between the ages of 4 and 6 were at risk of becoming street children. This has been changed by persuading such children to attend a pre-school centre set up by local volunteers. The results show two immediate benefits. The children have been dissuaded from dropping out into a life of crime and are better prepared for compulsory schooling which they start at the age of 7.

Guatemala City shows what can be achieved when those with responsibilities for urban management enter into dialogue with local people and international agencies. A partnership involving local, national and international organisations has certainly borne fruit. Much has been achieved by a large input of directed self-help.

Review

10 Revise the diagram **3.3** to show the urban management system in the South.

11 With reference to the Guatemala City case study, show how progress on one front might help progress on others.

Enquiry

Through the Internet, collect information on:
a one Urban Development Corporation
b one British new town.

In the case of (**a**), make an assessment of its particular aims and achievements so far.
In the case of (**b**), make an assessment of its achievements and shortcomings.

4

Turning the city inside out

The aim of this chapter is to identify recent changes affecting the face of cities in the North. Presumably these changes are part of the move towards a more thoroughly post-industrial city. For our purposes, the city is simply divided into three zones – the centre, the inner city and the suburbs. Having identified the changes, we need to ask two related questions:

■ Are these changes merely altering the relative importance of the different parts of the city?
■ Or do they represent important steps towards an entirely different urban structure?

Whilst the focus throughout this chapter is on the MEDCs, particularly the UK, some attempt is made to assess the situation in the cities of the South.

SECTION A

The suburban scene

It might appear perverse, but we should take the three zones in reverse order. This can be justified by the fact that the suburbs are where much of the action is. Growth is being stimulated from two different directions – from outside by new businesses and residents, and from the city centre and inner city by people and businesses moving out.

Figure 4.1 Newcomers to post-industrial suburbia

The suburbs are the outer and contiguous areas of a city. Traditionally, they were predominantly residential, but this has now changed (**4.1**). While suburbs are the creation of advances in transport, for many of their residents they represent a sort of compromise. That compromise is between the wish to have an urban job and access to city services, and the wish to live in areas that have an air of rurality about them. The rural essence is conjured up by the garden, the public park and physical nearness to the countryside. An additional consideration is the availability in the suburbs of housing with all modern amenities and built to exacting standards.

Perhaps the most outstanding feature of the post-industrial suburb in Britain and Western Europe has been the influx of non-residential land uses (**4.1**). The suburbs have become the destination for much retailing, many offices and those remaining manufacturing plants, all decentralising from central and inner-city locations. These relocated activities are appearing in new modes, such as huge edge- and out-of-town shopping complexes, office and business parks, industrial estates and so on (see **Case study**, **Chapter 5 Section B**). Some wholly new firms are supplementing the suburban industrial base formed by manufacturers that have relocated from the inner city. These are engaged mainly in the service and high-tech sectors. All these non-residential newcomers have been drawn to the suburbs by the same general attractions of cheaper sites, more space, better road access and nearness to the right sort of labour pools. In addition, the suburbs, particularly their fringes, are able to offer more pleasant working and living environments.

Edge cities

The decentralisation of so much commercial and industrial development to the outer margins of North American cities now has immense momentum. Most of these activities have decentralised in order to escape the high costs (land, labour recruitment, crime, etc.) of the central and inner city. The decentralisation is so great that it has prompted some observers to announce the 'end of suburbia'. The point being made is that in the 1990s some suburbs have matured into places with city-like qualities. The juxtaposing of office blocks, factories, huge shopping complexes and 'normal' suburban residential development is converting parts of the suburbs into something that more closely approaches a city.

The term **edge city** is increasingly used to label these new nucleations in the outer suburbs. They are seen to be a diagnostic feature of **post-suburban** America which has been described as:

fragmented, multi-nodal, with mixed densities and unexpected juxtapositions of form and function... It is also characterised by packaged landscapes – big set-piece developments such as waterfront improvements, festival marketplaces, gallerias, science parks, office villages and private master-planned communities.
Knox, 1992

See the following case studies.

The nuclei of edge cities (aptly described as **suburban downtowns**) are typically located near airports and freeway intersections. Often they are physically detached from the edge of the city's built-up area. Many of them do not have official names that show up on maps or in guidebooks. Knox has said:

In many respects they are 'stealth' cities, invisible administratively and politically, without their own chambers of commerce, libraries, town halls, public squares or courthouses.

Case study: Tysons Corner (Virginia) – a stealth city

In the mid-1960s Tysons Corner was nothing more than a rural area, but it did happen to be located by the intersection of the important freeway Interstate 66 and the toll road to Dulles International Airport. Today, urban development around this accessible point now covers an area of 2400 ha; it houses 30 000 people and provides 75 000 jobs. Perhaps because the site was originally split between three counties, Tysons Corner today still lacks any sort of autonomy. This is all the more amazing bearing in mind that this is now the ninth largest concentration of commercial space in the USA. It covers an area of more than 2 million m^2, including several million m^2 of retail space, more than 3000 hotel rooms, and parking for more than 80 000 cars. But for all this and the personal affluence that goes with it, Tysons Corner has no public open space, no recreation centres, no bus stops and few social services.

Tysons Corner is an example of awesome growth. Equally, it is the object of scorn because of its low standards of design, its unplanned nature and its lack of civic status. Tysons Corner is an example of the new, post-suburban, multi-centric metropolitan form. It poses a whole range of social, political and planning issues. Is the planning situation in the UK sufficiently different to ensure that edge and stealth cities remain on the other side of the Atlantic?

Case study: Avenel, Maryland

A new residential form is appearing around the margins of the North American city, often as part of emerging edge cities. They are carefully-planned and privately-built developments for the affluent or middle-class buyer. They are acknowledged as being an integral part of **post-suburban** America.

Avenel, located in suburban Maryland close to Washington, is one of them. It is a 400ha development of more than 800 homes set in a luxuriously landscaped area. This green space includes a golf course, an equestrian centre and bridle trails, open parkland and a recreational park with tennis courts, soccer pitches and jogging trails. It is a 'garden city' in all but size and name, and an up-market one at that. Dwellings are large and set in extensive grounds. They currently fetch prices approaching $1 million. Typically in such developments, there is a preoccupation with security and surveillance, and a determination to remain remote from the crime, violence and drugs that plague nearby cities. The range of service varies, but most communities enjoy the basics such as an elementary school, medical centre, etc. Because of their distinctive architecture, lavish landscape and personal security, Avenel and other master-planned communities like it are fast becoming part of the middle-American dream. They are in effect, up-market new towns.

Review

1 Account for the dynamic nature of today's suburbia.

2 With reference to the Avenel case study, outline what you see as the advantages and disadvantages of living in an edge city.

Edge cities are unlikely to become a British phenomenon, mainly because of the impact of the green belts and tighter planning controls (see **Chapter 6 Sections B and C**). In the British case, it is probably more appropriate to talk in terms of a **spread city**, particularly along major transport corridors. Tentacles of discontinuous development reach out from London along motorways such as the M1, M3, M4 and M11.

SECTION B

Inner-city despair

The traditional image of the inner city is of an area dominated by high-density and rather obsolete housing, much of it terraced and constructed during the 19th century. It was accommodation intended primarily for working-class residents. Subsequently, it has provided homes for newly-arrived immigrants. In many cities, the housing grew up around factories which have since closed down or relocated to the suburbs. In this stereotyped image, we can begin to identify some of the inherent problems of the inner city:

- deteriorating and often substandard housing
- a loss of jobs
- better-off households moving out
- declining services
- consolidation of city poor and ethnic minorities.

The downward spiral

Clearly, these problems are interrelated in a sort of **downward spiral** (4.2). It starts with the outward movement of better-off families and major users of urban land such as industry and wholesaling. This reduces the amount of money that local authorities can collect by way of taxes. The loss of urban activities such as industry and wholesaling increases the level of unemployment. This in turn creates personal financial difficulties for those people left behind (the unskilled, the elderly and immigrants). Public services deteriorate in quality, especially education which is vital to personal improvement. Housing deteriorates and is characterised by

Figure 4.2 Components in the downward spiral of inner-city decline

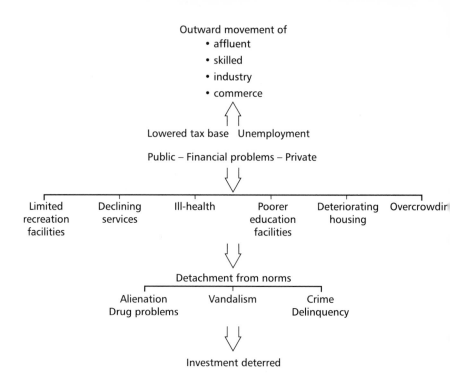

Outward movement of
- affluent
- skilled
- industry
- commerce

Lowered tax base   Unemployment

Public – Financial problems – Private

| Limited recreation facilities | Declining services | Ill-health | Poorer education facilities | Deteriorating housing | Overcrowding |

Detachment from norms

| Alienation Drug problems | Vandalism | Crime Delinquency |

Investment deterred

overcrowding. Health problems tend to become more severe. There are few local recreational opportunities. In these conditions, the younger people, in particular, begin to feel that they are being left behind and discriminated against. Thus they become alienated, turning away from the accepted or normal way of life. This leads to all forms of anti-social behaviour, such as drug-taking, hooliganism, vandalism and crime. This unfavourable social climate has a knock-on effect by driving out still more businesses and so raising unemployment and lowering tax revenue. So the downward spiral continues.

Cycle of poverty

The downward spiral therefore creates an environment of decay and despair for a range of people who collectively form what is known as the **urban underclass**. For them, it may be right to talk in terms of an **inner-city crisis**. At a personal level, many are victims of a self-perpetuating **cycle of poverty** (4.3). This is thought to occur because of the interdependence of unskilled jobs, low incomes, poor living conditions and poor educational opportunities. The cycle is transmitted from one generation to the next. The children of poor parents receive little parental support and are forced to attend inadequate schools. As a result, they leave school at the earliest possible opportunity and with few qualifications. This, in turn, means that there are difficulties in finding work and that they can only expect to earn low wages for doing rather menial tasks. Thus they remain 'trapped' in a cycle of poverty and are largely powerless to improve their lot. Their impeded access to good housing, a secure and well-paid job and adequate services means that they are victims of **multiple deprivation**.

Figure 4.3 The cycle of poverty

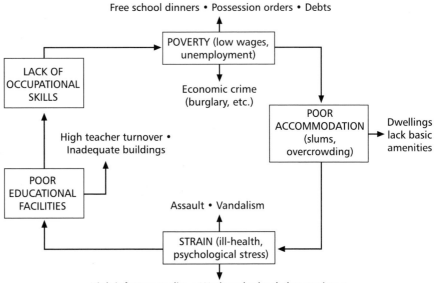

Free school dinners • Possession orders • Debts

POVERTY (low wages, unemployment)

LACK OF OCCUPATIONAL SKILLS

Economic crime (burglary, etc.)

POOR ACCOMMODATION (slums, overcrowding)

Dwellings lack basic amenities

High teacher turnover • Inadequate buildings

POOR EDUCATIONAL FACILITIES

Assault • Vandalism

STRAIN (ill-health, psychological stress)

High infant mortality • Work and school absenteeism • Children in care • Mental illness • Maladjustment • Suicide

Discrimination

Reference has just been made to the fact that people in the inner city feel discriminated against. There is perhaps another dimension to that discrimination. The evidence is provided by the **ghetto** – the concentration of ethnic minorities in particular parts of this generally disadvantaged zone. It is quite clear that newly-arrived immigrants make for the inner city, principally because it offers the cheapest accommodation. Equally, members of the same ethnic group are happy to agglomerate in the same area for feelings of security and cultural affinity. The concern is that once the ghetto pattern is established, it tends to persist. Is it by choice or force of circumstance? Here there are two irreconcilable schools of thought. Whatever the answer might be, it is important to recognise that the ghetto can serve three different roles:

- It can be the means by which the identity and distinctiveness of an immigrant ethnic group may be preserved in an 'alien' environment.
- It can provide the base from which an ethnic minority gradually disperses into the host society and undergoes a degree of assimilation.
- It can be the means by which an ethnic minority is prevented from dispersing and merging with the host population.

Figure **4.4** models a number of different scenarios for the ghetto once it is formed. Basically, three different contingencies are anticipated. In the first, the ghetto remains in its original location, either growing (A) or remaining static (B). In the second, the ghetto shifts location, most likely because the economic position of the minority group improves (C). In all three models the ghetto is preserved. In three remaining scenarios, there is significant assimilation and the ghetto disperses. In D there is a loss of spatial identity.

Figure 4.4 Models of ghetto evolution

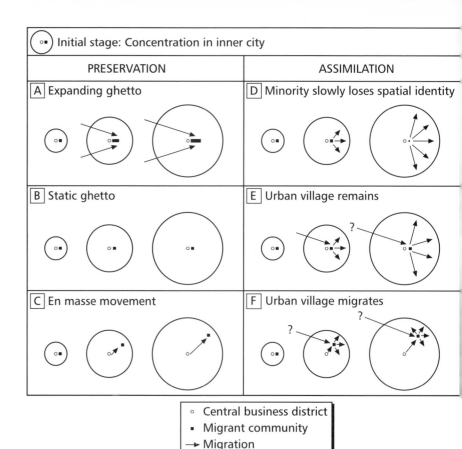

In **E**, although there is assimilation, members of the group still loosely associate in what are termed **urban villages**. In **F** the urban village is strengthened by new migrants, but because individual circumstances are so improved, the village as a whole moves to a newer residential area. These last two models are well illustrated by the movements of the Jewish community in London (**4.5**).

Figure 4.5 The movement of the Jewish community in London

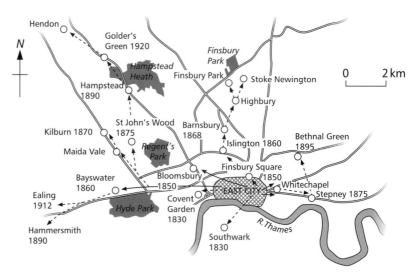

Case study: Immigrant patterns and behaviour in Sydney

Sydney today is a city of over 3.5 million inhabitants. Possibly as many as a half of them were born outside Australia. During the second half of the 20th century, Sydney functioned as a giant melting-pot drawing in immigrants from different parts of the world. Initially, most came from the British Isles. There then followed great waves of immigration from southern and eastern Europe. Recently, the countries of Asia have become major suppliers of new residents. Sydney's immigrant mix involves differences of race, religion and nationality.

The residential pattern adopted by immigrant groups is conditioned by ethnic and national ties, as well as the niche they are able to find in the social hierarchy. Most immigrants still make the inner city their first home, where there is a noticeable spatial segregation of different groups. However, the stay there is typically a short one – a year or two – and relocation to newer residential areas soon follows. The outward movement leads to dispersal and varying degrees of assimilation. Even so, a journey through the outer suburbs of Sydney today will reveal pockets where particular groups are still inclined to cluster. It says much for cosmopolitan Sydney that there is much tolerance and little discrimination.

Regeneration

At this stage, we need to be careful, and recognise that we have been dealing in generalisations about the inner city, and potentially dangerous ones at that. It would be wrong to see the whole of the inner city as a great 'sea of despair'. **Economic decay** and **social dislocation** have a patchy occurrence. They also occur elsewhere in the city, most notably in the peripheral post-war council housing estates (see **5.2**). We should also recognise that a range of initiatives have been taken to improve inner-city conditions.

Let us now look briefly at two different examples of **urban regeneration** effort. First, there have been many **urban renewal** programmes. These have focused on physical regeneration, and targeted housing and the residential environment. In the 1950s and 1960s, regeneration meant **redevelopment** involving what became known as the **bulldozer approach**. Old and substandard housing was simply demolished and replaced, usually by high-rise blocks of flats. Eventually, city authorities became aware of the social dislocation and costs associated with demolition and stacking people vertically. Thus in the 1970s there began a gradual shift of emphasis towards **improvement** rather than clearance. More recently, a start has been made on replacing the unloved high-rise apartment blocks by more conventional two-storey dwellings. With all three types of residential regeneration, there is an element of displacement. This arises because the number of people who can be rehoused *in situ* is most frequently lower than the number of pre-regeneration residents.

Gentrification

Gentrification, the second form of inner-city regeneration, is the movement of affluent, usually young, middle-class people into run-down inner-city areas. The eventual outcome is a social upgrading alongside an improvement of property and the residential environment. More money circulates locally and this encourages an upgrading of local services. How gentrification starts is an interesting question. Is it triggered by chance, or by spontaneous decisions taken by a few people? Or is it led (one might say, contrived) by speculative developers or local authorities? It is possible that evidence may be found to support all three explanations. We can be a little more certain about what motivates the people who are drawn to gentrified areas. Considerations include:

- nearness to the city centre for work, shops, entertainment and leisure opportunities
- good public transport
- preference for older styles of housing
- the prospect of better local services (particularly schools and medical centres) created by the coming together of more affluent households
- the buzz of living in an upwardly mobile area.

Once started, gentrification can gather quite a momentum leading to possible **trickle-down effects** in adjacent areas. They have the potential to become cores of inner-city revival. But there are costs, largely of a social kind. For example, a degree of social disharmony is inevitably created between the newcomers and the existing working-class residents. Gentrification leads to a rise in house prices. Existing residents can cash in on their unimproved dwellings, but find they cannot then afford to buy improved properties in the same area. Thus there is an element of spatial displacement.

Case study: 'Urban regeneration fuels Birmingham's boom'

This was the banner headline of a recent newspaper article. The article claimed that 'Birmingham, Britain's second city, has undergone intensive urban regeneration, and estate agents say that it is paying off... New Birmingham is brighter and safer, and the once decrepit inner city has been transformed into a desirable place to live.'

This achievement is the result of five years of regeneration. It is the outcome of a combination of EU money and the efforts of non-government organisations. It has been helped by the presence nearby of prestige developments such as the National Indoor Arena and the International Convention Centre located on the margins of the central-city area. It involves a new approach to urban planning in response to a rising demand for homes near the city centre. In the past, planning was about the segregation of different urban land uses. Here the planners have aimed at creating 'urban villages' where these activities are mixed. The approach creates a community where people can live and work. One of these is at Brindleyplace where there is a blend of homes, offices, shops and leisure facilities.

The creation of some of these 'villages' has involved converting commercial properties into residential accommodation. For example, the former British Telecom Tower has been transformed into 65 one- and two-bedroom flats, with prices in 1998 ranging from £75 000 to £225 000. Another example is provided by the conversion of the old Royal Mail building.

The comments of someone who has returned from the countryside and bought a flat in the BT Tower scheme is revealing:

Until recently, there was nowhere in central Birmingham where it was safe to live. But that has changed and there has been real regeneration. It is cleaner, safer and more pedestrianised. Old buildings have been given a facelift. It had a reputation for being drab and run-down, but that has changed. My apartment is ultra-modern, with a high-quality specification in what is now a good area.

There is no doubt that some run-down, desolate urban wastelands in Birmingham have been changed into sophisticated modern developments. The recycling of redundant buildings, the cleaning-up of canals and other open spaces and the use of 'brown' sites are all to be applauded. So too is the return of residential social groups who deserted the area in the past. The questions have to be asked – what has all this done to reduce deprivation and discrimination? Is this anything more than gentrification?

Brownfield sites

Over the years, the inner city has been a supply base for decentralisation. It has despatched people, jobs and services to the suburbs. As a consequence, space has been vacated and land values have dropped. The presence of derelict buildings and vacant weed-ridden land is not good for the image of the inner city. The argument is made that using and redeveloping these 'brown' or **brownfield sites** should have priority over greenfield sites in the countryside. It is a persuasive argument and it conjures up interesting images of waves of new suburban growth rippling back into the inner city rather than invading rural space.

Case study: A brown and unpleasant land

More than 100km² of England's green countryside – that is an area the size of Bristol – is built over every year. England has lost an area of countryside almost the size of Wales since the 1960s. If this rate of loss continues, one-fifth of England will be urban by 2050. Yet there are nearly 600km² of unused land in urban England which could be built on instead. At present, the government and county authorities seem to be giving in to the greenfield developers rather than insisting that idle urban space is recycled. See **Chapter 6 Section C**.

The so-called **inner-city crisis** is nothing new. Philanthropists and reformers in Britain and elsewhere were drawing attention to the symptoms even in the second half of the 19th century. The worry is that despite 100 years of awareness and action, the despair is no less; indeed, it seems to be getting even worse. We will return to one aspect of this whole issue of the inner city in **Chapter 5 Section B**.

Review

3 Try to arrange the components shown in **4.2** into a downward spiral. Where do you start and finish?

4 What do you understand by the following terms: **downward spiral, cycle of poverty, ghetto, urban regeneration, gentrification, brownfield site**?

5 State the three possible roles of the ghetto. Which role do you think has been most followed in the UK?

6 Distinguish between **redevelopment** and **improvement**.

7 What are your answers to the two questions at the end of the Birmingham case study? (page 49)

8 Suggest some difficulties that might be associated with using brownfield rather than greenfield sites.

City-centre survival

Reference has already been made to the shopping centres, business and office parks at the urban fringe. To a considerable degree these have been filled by firms originally located in the city centre. Clearly, their loss has been a serious blow to the general well-being of the city centre. Their departure was encouraged by traffic congestion, high land values and unattractive urban landscapes, often the product of poor architecture and planning. Fears about personal safety helped to ensure desertion of the city centre after dark.

It was during the property boom of the 1980s that the city centre began to fight back. This was particularly the case in those cities with suburbs spilling over into adjacent local authority areas. Here, decentralisation from the centre means losing valuable revenue and jobs to another local government area. From amongst a wide range of initiatives aimed at reviving the city centre, four are illustrated in the Southampton case study.

Case study: Southampton – the centre fights back

Southampton City Council has supported a number of actions all designed to protect the well-being of the city centre. Special circumstances persuading them to do this have been:

- the inaccessibility of the city centre due to its location close to the tip of a peninsula (**4.6**)
- the movement of the CBD northwards away from the historic walled town
- the fundamental change in the make-up of port traffic, from passengers to containerised cargo; redundant dock installations have released much waterside space
- a lack of space left within its boundaries to allow edge-of-town developments.

Listed below are some of the more recent actions with their specific aims and achievements (**4.6**).

Flagship developments

Aim: To improve the image of the city centre.
Projects
- Ocean Village – a large marina development with housing and leisure facilities
- Southampton Oceanography Centre – one of the world's top ocean research institutions
- West Quay – the largest project of its kind currently being built in Europe (shops, leisure, business and community facilities)

Festival events

Aims: To raise the city's profile and to bring visitors to the city centre.
Projects
- Southampton Boat Show – the largest of its kind in the UK
- Ordnance Survey Balloon and Flower Festival
- Whitbread Round the World Race

Shopping malls

Aims: To create a pleasant shopping environment and to keep together a range of good-quality shops.

Figure 4.6 Recent major developments in central Southampton

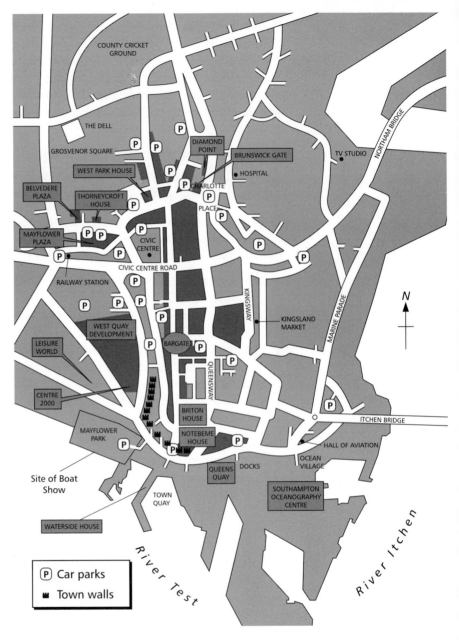

Projects
- The Bargate Centre
- The Marlands Centre
- West Quay Retail Park – see page 51

Office space

Aims: To ensure that the city remains a major office centre and attracts office relocations from other parts of the UK.

Projects
- Mayflower Plaza –18 500m^2 of space, plus Arts Centre
- Queens Quay – a huge 2.42ha development
- Belvedere Place – 6050m^2 of space

Leisure facilities

Aim: To increase the city's leisure opportunities for all.
Project
- Centre 2000 – a large swimming and diving centre, nearing completion

Road improvements

Aims: To overcome the inaccessibility of the city centre and to lower the level of private car use.
Projects
- M271 motorway spur, Western approach road and Portswood link feed to city centre
- 20 mph speed limit in city centre
- Car parking – good provision, but charges apply
- Park and ride – operates at Christmas and during major events only

Conserving heritage

Aims: To conserve the special character of the walled town and to attract visitors.
Projects
- Town walls and Bargate
- Tudor Museum

There is no official boundary to the city centre. The location of some of the projects might be seen as lying within the fringe between city centre and inner city.

Heritage and recycling

Diagram **4.7** summarises some of the regeneration changes and opportunities taking place in and around city centres. **Recycling** is a buzzword these days, but it is certainly appropriate to describe much of what is going on by way of urban regeneration. Recycling has two targets: land and buildings. The former usually involves redevelopment. Vacated sites are cleared and made ready for new buildings and new uses (the **brownfield sites**).

More challenging is the recycling of old buildings. Normally this involves subtly and sympathetically changing and improving them so that they can accommodate new uses. This type of recycling by improvement, as illustrated in the Birmingham case study (page 48), finds much favour at present. It is part of a much wider movement that sees great value in our **urban heritage** of buildings and spaces. Conserving historic urban fabric enhances the quality of the urban landscape. It not only adds character, but also gives a sense of continuity and community.

It is now realised that a concern for urban heritage is not just something for historic cities like Bath, Chester and York. All cities should be aware of it, decide what is best and take appropriate action. In the case of Southampton, despite extensive bomb damage during the Second World

Figure 4.7 Typology of central- and inner-city regeneration

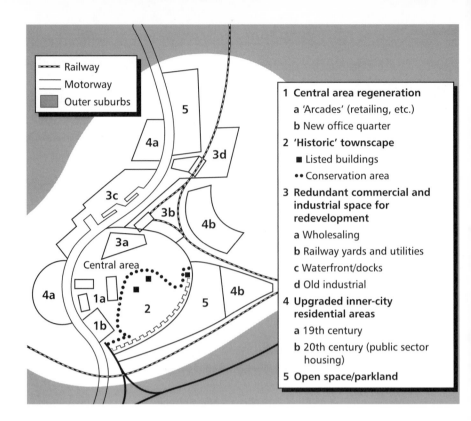

Legend:
- ▰▰▰ Railway
- ▭ Motorway
- ▨ Outer suburbs

1 Central area regeneration
  a 'Arcades' (retailing, etc.)
  b New office quarter

2 'Historic' townscape
  ■ Listed buildings
  •• Conservation area

3 Redundant commercial and industrial space for redevelopment
  a Wholesaling
  b Railway yards and utilities
  c Waterfront/docks
  d Old industrial

4 Upgraded inner-city residential areas
  a 19th century
  b 20th century (public sector housing)

5 Open space/parkland

War, much has been done to preserve the walls of the old medieval town. There is no doubt that this adds something to the city centre. There is also an economic spin-off, because historic urban fabric often attracts tourists.

Review

9 Try to relate the developments in the centre of Southampton to the typology in **4.7**.

10 Itemise the benefits associated with preserving urban heritage. What challenges does it pose?

SECTION D

A changing balance

What might we conclude from this brief look at what is happening in the three zones of the post-industrial city? Clearly, there are signs of change, but there is nothing new in that. City structures have always been fairly dynamic and sensitive to changing pressures and processes. The signs at this time suggest that urban form is moving away from the long-established centripetal pattern of a strong centre. This is hardly surprising, because to continue to focus on one point can only result in congestion and acute competition for space. All this greatly raises costs.

Review

11 Sketch a model diagram to show what you think will be the key features of the 'polo-mint' city.

12 Construct a matrix comparing the advantages and disadvantages of a 'polo-mint' city and a 'strong-centred' city.

13 What is your answer to the question about the urban managers?

'Strong-centred' cities were encouraged by yesterday's transport modes and networks. There was much greater reliance on public transport. Vastly increased private car-ownership and the use of the car for work, leisure and seeking services have set in motion a fundamental shift in the balance of forces. This change in the transport situation, together with advances in telecommunications, now encourage a much looser urban form and indeed offer the prospect of massive decentralisation on a spatial scale that reaches beyond the suburbs (see **Chapter 6**).

What we see at the moment is a telling combination:

- a weakening of central-city status
- a continuing stagnation and decline of the inner city and
- an increasing dynamism in the suburbs.

We might be forgiven for anticipating a new urban form. Do we call it the post-industrial end-form? Towns and cities seem to be turning inside out and perhaps assuming a 'polo-mint' structure. The shift in this direction is most marked in the cities of free-market economies, particularly the USA. The evidence there lies in the massive abandonment of the CBD and the mush-rooming of edge cities. In the mixed economies of the North, where there is much more intervention in the form of planning, there is a degree of resistance to the forces of change. Attempts have been made to revive or protect city centres, rehabilitate the inner city and contain the suburbs. But what are the responsibilities of the urban managers – to resist or assist change?

A view from the South

Cities in LEDCs are no less dynamic than their counterparts in the North. Perhaps they are more so. However, a shorter history and a faster pace of urbanisation, together with differences in economic and social conditions, have created some distinctive urban forms. The LEDC city is above all a 'strong-centred' city. The CBD is unchallenged as the hub and has not experienced any significant decentralisation. Its character is summed up in the three Cs – commerce, congestion and chaos. It is outside the CBD that differences begin to appear.

Immediately beyond the CBD, instead of moving into a twilight zone of run-down housing and deprivation, we can find a rather different urban landscape. It usually dates from pre-industrial or colonial times. It contains the spacious and luxurious homes that were originally built for wealthy landowners, prosperous merchants and powerful administrators. Some of the original dwellings have deteriorated in condition and been cleared, but they have been replaced by modern high-rise apartments. Much of this belt continues to be home to the wealthy, who value nearness to the city centre and the prestige of living in an ambient historic quarter. Here and there, some blighting has occurred and the wealthy have left. This has happened where main roads and railways cut through to the CBD and where industry has gained a footing. Sectors of change are formed.

The next zone out is characterised by rather poor-quality housing. Much of it was built by the original occupants in a distinctly spontaneous manner. Construction of the necessary infrastructure of water and power supplies and sewage disposal is very much a second-phase activity. Large areas remain unserviced.

The outer belt mainly comprises the shanty or squatter developments that tend to provide the first homes for rural–urban migrants. Such accommodation lacks the basic amenities. Living conditions are distinctly unhealthy and disease prevails. But it would be wrong to think that this belt is exclusively one of slum housing. Those more wealthy people who have decided to leave the inner belt are frequently to be found here. Typically, they seek out desirable sites, as on high ground or along coastal stretches; they cluster into distinct communities and protect their families and homes inside heavily guarded compounds.

Case study: Port Moresby, Papua New Guinea

Figure 4.8 Port Moresby

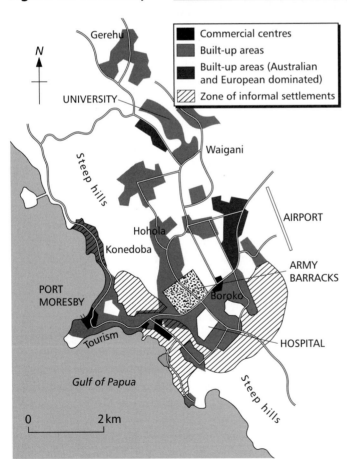

Port Moresby, the capital city of Papua New Guinea, was founded as the seat of British colonial government in 1886. The coastal site was chosen because of its good potential for the development of a port. Even as late as 1961, the population of the town was less than 30 000. Today it has exploded to over 175 000.

The commercial centre of the early town in the port is now remote from the modern built-up area (4.8). The latter has spread eastwards towards the International Airport and northwards in the direction of the University. The old town is separated from the 'new' Port Moresby by a marked escarpment. The layout of the new built-up area on the upland surface is made up of interlinked suburban tracts but separated by open space. Squatter or informal settlements are conspicuous in the gap between the old and new towns and there is a great sweep of them around the southern side of the built-up area. It is here that many of the **villager immigrants** have found accommodation.

A particular problem in these shanty areas is the simmering resentment among members of rival tribal groups. Out in the country, they are at open war with each other. In Port Moresby, they are forced to quash their warring instincts and try to be tolerant. What with this, and the fact that they come from areas that are still in the Stone Age, the urban environment must seem a very puzzling place. It is hardly surprising that crime, alcoholism and drug addiction have taken root. Deprivation certainly exists, but it does not compare with the state of affairs back in the villages.

The two areas of good housing are related to the Airport (with some service industry) and the University. Both areas contain significant numbers of Australian and European residents. The old colonial area down by the coast is slowly being abandoned by more wealthy families. Some of the villas have been converted into guest houses; others have been replaced by purpose-built hotels and office blocks. There are now at least three commercial centres, but the oldest one down at the port maintains its premier position.

Review

14 Draw a diagram to show the essential features of the LEDC city as described in the text.

15 How does the structure of Port Moresby compare with that portrayed in your model of the LEDC city?

Enquiry

1 Select one of the motorways leading out of London. Find out what new developments have taken place during the last 10 to 15 years along or close to that stretch lying within a 100km radius of the centre of London. What sorts of activity are involved? To what extent are they London-oriented or motorway-oriented? What is there to stop the formation of a single tentacle of urban development?

2 For a town that you know at first hand, find out what parts (if any) have been designated or listed for conservation. How and why were those particular areas chosen?

Inside city issues

In this chapter, the spotlight falls on three of the most pressing problems inside today's towns and cities. It would take a huge volume to examine in detail all the difficulties and deficiencies that mark today's built-up area. The approach in this chapter therefore has to be selective and concise. The problems chosen are closely related.

- Improving the quality of life and the built environment.
- The complex and taxing issue of housing the city's poor.
- The challenge of keeping the city moving.

All three issues involve discrimination and inequality. Together they form a powerful force behind the decentralisation that characterises the post-industrial city.

Public awareness of these problems is raised by the frequency and degree to which they are exposed by today's mass-media. Whether public understanding is improved is another matter. Whilst these are major urban issues in the North, an attempt is made here to assess whether their character and importance are the same in the South.

SECTION A

Quality of life and the built environment

The huge flood of people from the inner city to the suburb has been a conspicuous theme in earlier chapters. **Chapter 6** will show how the outward ripple continues from the suburbs deep into rural space. As with most migrations, both legs of this decentralisation have been a response to push factors. A powerful factor has been personal dissatisfaction. Some of that dissatisfaction and the decision to move is specifically related to housing (**Section B**) and the difficulties of moving around the city (**Section C**). Important though they are, they are only part of a much wider appraisal that is being made by people about their living conditions. The **quality of life** is a key concept here.

Quality of life

Anyone's quality of life is a multi-faceted condition. It is the outcome of a range of interacting factors. The Organisation for Economic Co-operation and Development (OECD) has listed over 20 criteria under 8 major headings (**5.1**). The scheme underlines a key feature identified in the previous chapter: the close interdependence of factors that impinge on our everyday lives.

Figure 5.1 OECD's measures of quality of life

Health – probability of good health throughout life-cycle

Education – acquisition of knowledge, skills and values for good citizenship

Employment – job satisfaction, level of remuneration

Time and leisure – freedom of choice in the use of time

Goods and services – accessibility, range of choice and quality

Physical environment – quality of housing, levels of pollution

Personal safety – violence, victimisation, harassment and justice

Social opportunity – social inequality, participation in community life

Any evaluation of the quality of life has to take into account the particular tastes and perceptions of the individual. It is very much a personal matter. However, from a sample of individuals in different parts of the city, it is possible to derive an aggregate picture. High mean scores signal prevalence of the 'good life'. Low mean scores flag up deprivation. Studies of British cities have shown that mean quality of life scores often fall below minimum acceptable levels in three types of urban area:

Figure 5.2 The distribution of deprived areas in Stoke-on-Trent

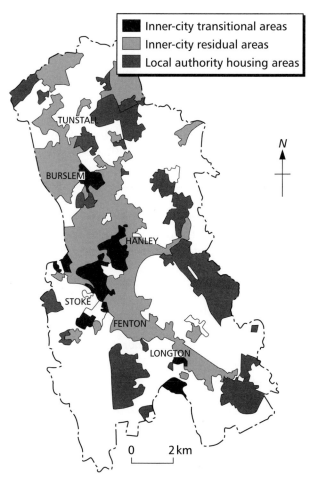

Inner-city transitional areas
Inner-city residual areas
Local authority housing areas

TUNSTALL

BURSLEM

HANLEY

STOKE

FENTON

LONGTON

N

0   2 km

- **Inner-city transitional areas** where houses are subdivided into flats and bed-sits and where there is a high incidence of young adults and immigrants. These are areas of the industrial city that once housed better-off households who have since abandoned them.
- **Inner-city residual areas** where old owner-occupied terraced housing accommodates an older population of medium to low social status. These too are relic areas of the industrial city.
- **Local authority housing areas** where rented accommodation is mainly occupied by people of low social status. These are areas, often close to the city margins, that have been built to accommodate poorer households (see **Case study** on page 65).

Map **5.2** shows the occurrence of such areas in Stoke-on-Trent. The pattern here is complicated by the fact that five once-separate towns have grown together to form today's built-up area. Here we are seeing the spatial sorting of people who are caught up in the cycle of poverty (see **Chapter 4 Section B**).

It is important to stress the point that council estates are not all the same. Most local government authorities tend to reserve at least one of their estates for disruptive 'difficult' families – the so-called **sink estates**. The differences between estates were also increased during the 1980s with the 'right to buy' scheme. Better-off tenants were given the opportunity to buy their homes. This led to a noticeable physical and social upgrading of a significant number of estates.

Case study: Hit-squads to fight urban poverty

In October 1998 the government announced that six of Britain's worst poverty trouble-spots had been identified as targets for an all-out attack on social dislocation and a special promotion of health, education and employment. The plan is for teams of civil servants to oversee a series of regeneration initiatives in Newcastle upon Tyne, Plymouth, South Yorkshire, East London, Sandwell and West Cumbria. These schemes will co-ordinate the efforts of three existing area-based initiatives – Health and Education Action Zones, Employment Zones and the New Deal for Communities. This is to ensure that they complement each other and do not cover the same ground.

The new units will work across local and central government departments. They will also consult with community representatives and interest groups to identify the best ways of approaching regeneration in their area. It is recognised that long-term problems such as ill-health, poor education, inadequate housing and unemployment are interrelated. They need to be tackled by this sort of single overarching strategy. Only time will tell whether they are successful or whether any useful lessons can be learned from the experiment.

Quality of the built environment

This is really an inseparable ingredient of the quality of life. For the moment, though, let us examine it in isolation. Criteria to assess the physical quality of the built environment might include:

- the quality, condition and layout of housing
- the availability of safe water and waste disposal
- the levels of air and water pollution
- the ratio of green or open space to bricks and concrete
- the incidence of noise, obnoxious smells and unsightliness
- the efficiency and ease of movement.

Case study: Environmental problems in Rio de Janeiro

By 1995 the population of Rio de Janeiro's metropolitan area of 6500km^2 had grown to over 10 million. The main environmental problems associated with this remarkable growth include:

- **Water pollution** – contamination of streams and coastal waters by inadequately treated domestic sewage and industrial effluent from oil-refining, petrochemicals, chemicals, iron and steel and other metal-refining industries.
- **Air pollution** – coming from the same industrial sources, and from heavy motor vehicle traffic. The relief of the metropolitan site and prevailing wind direction can help concentrate pollutants.
- **The rapid and uncontrolled expansion of the built-up area**, often over unsafe land at the margins of the city. The metropolitan area lacks powers to ensure that fragile slopes are properly protected and that housing is serviced with safe water and waste disposal facilities.
- **The deforestation of slopes** leading to instability and erosion, particularly during summer rains. Landslides are commonplace; stream channels become choked with soil and debris and thereby increase the flood hazard.
- **The incapacity of the metropolitan government to manage** the vast quantity of solid and liquid wastes generated within the metropolitan area.

Rio has enjoyed a worldwide reputation for the natural beauty of its site. Beaches, such as those around Guanabara Bay, have proved to be an important amenity for local residents as well as an economic asset in tourism. Sadly, all that is now seriously threatened by Rio's growing ecological footprint.

Case study: Environmental problems in Bangkok

Bangkok is a city in crisis. As recently as the early 1960s, when its population was 1.5 million, the city had a reputation as the 'Venice of the East'. It was criss-crossed by a network of canals or *klongs*; these played an important role in the life of the city. Today, the population is fast approaching the 7 million mark. The *klongs* have mostly been filled in or are used as open sewers. The unplanned mushrooming of the city has created a host of environmental problems.

- Today there are some 300 **slum areas** scattered throughout the city. In all, they provide shelter for over 1 million people. The largest is Kiong Toey (**5.3**) where 40 000 people live in what has been described as 'a shrinking area of tin and wooden shacks over a stinking swamp of black mud, untreated sewage and rotting rubbish'.

Figure 5.3 Kiong Toey – slum housing

- Probably as much as half of Bangkok's **water supply** is lost through broken pipes. Half the city's population relies on wells and pumps that tend to suck up contaminated water. At least 100 000 residents draw on the Chao Praya River for their water supply. The river is massively polluted.
- The problem of disposing of household and human **waste** is huge. There is no sewage disposal system. On top of all this is the effluent produced by the city's growing number of factories.
- There are high levels of **air pollution** caused by huge volumes of motor traffic, much traffic congestion and unregulated industrial development. Noise and obnoxious smells are other environmental problems.
- **Flooding** is a real hazard. Because of the massive pumping of underground water, the city is sinking by 10 cm every year. The city is only about one metre above sea-level. Given the present levels of pumping and rising sea-levels due to global warming, the whole city could be below sea-level in little more than 20 years.

The quality of the built-up area can produce important **externalities** or side-effects. A poor-quality environment is likely to produce **negative externalities** such as ill-health and disease. Another is the high incidence of **social malaise** (crime, delinquency, vandalism, drug addiction and mental illness). A good-quality environment, besides promising relative freedom from crime and vice, offers residents positive externalities such as stability, security, satisfaction and a general feeling of well-being.

Case study: Urban crime and violence

More than half the world's population living in cities with 100 000 or more inhabitants are victims, at least once every five years, of a crime of some kind (**5.4**).

Only in Asia does the proportion fall below 50 per cent, while in Africa and the Americas it is two-thirds or more. Table **5.4** shows that most crime is against property through theft, burglary and (not shown here) vandalism – a 'petty' crime which, along with hooliganism, often goes unreported. The increase in crime against property is not only a feature of rich neighbourhoods, but it is also spread within many low-income areas, including squatter settlements and shanties.

The rise in crimes of violence is a major cause for concern around the world. Murder, mugging, sexual assault, domestic violence and child

% of population who over a 5-year period are victims of ...					
	theft and damage of vehicles	burglary	other theft	assault and other crimes of personal attack	All crimes
Western Europe	34	16	27	15	60
North America	43	24	25	20	65
South America	25	20	33	31	68
Eastern Europe	27	18	28	17	56
Asia	12	13	25	11	44
Africa	24	38	42	33	76
Total	29	20	29	19	61

Figure 5.4 Victims of crime in cities larger than 100 000 over a period of five years

abuse are all on the increase. Most observers argue that the causes lie in the deprivation and discrimination that marks most, if not all, cities of the world.

It is important to appreciate that the knock-on effect of crime goes beyond the immediate victims. Rising crime creates a sense of insecurity. This in turn generates distrust, intolerance, and the withdrawal of people from community life. It also leads to intrusive surveillance as a form of protection. It is not uncommon for higher-income groups to live, work, shop and enjoy their leisure-time in what are basically fortified enclaves. See **Case studies, Chapter 4 Section A**.

Review

1 Give a definition of **quality of life** and suggest good ways to measure it.

2 Six indicators of the quality of the built environment are given on page 60. Can you suggest any others?

3 Compare the environmental problems of Rio de Janeiro and Bangkok. Which city do you think faces the greater challenge?

4 Describe what you think are the main environmental problems of the British city.

5 Write a short analytical account of the information contained in **5.4**.

Housing

Housing is a key ingredient in the **cycle of poverty** and the inner-city **downward spiral**. Secure, safe and adequately serviced housing is vital to everyone's quality of life and well-being. Having a roof over our heads is something that most of us take for granted. Yet housing is probably one of the most widespread and serious of all the problems facing today's cities, big or small, North or South. The so-called 'housing problem' has many different facets. Four aspects are particularly important:

- **The quality of housing** – its size, quality of construction, and servicing in terms of water, electricity and sewage disposal (**5.5**).
- **Housing tenure** – vital here is the proportion of households having protection against sudden and arbitrary eviction. In this respect, owner-occupiers have much greater security than those who rent or squat.
- **The quantity of housing** relative to the number of households – in urban areas demand often exceeds supply (**5.6**).
- **The accessibility of housing** – by this is meant the ease with which people are able to buy, rent or in other ways obtain housing.

Figure 5.5 Aspects of housing having important effects on health

* The structure of the dwelling – the extent to which it protects the occupants from damp and rain, extremes of heat and cold, noise, insects and rodents.

* The quality and quantity of water supply.

* The safe disposal of domestic waste.

* The degree of overcrowding – this is important in terms of household accidents, the transmission of airborne infections, the occurrence of pneumonia and tuberculosis.

* The generation of indoor pollution by the burning of fuels for cooking and heating.

* Food safety standards – protecting food against spoilage and contamination.

* The home as a workplace – the use and storage of toxic or hazardous chemicals; the safety of equipment.

Factors influencing housing demand	Factors influencing housing supply
Disposable income	Price and availability of land
Nature of employment	Price and availability of labour
Household priorities	Costs of materials, building and physical infrastructure
Availability of housing finance	Official standards on building, materials, services, etc.
Household age, size and structure	Extent to which illegal housing and land development are tolerated
Occupation	Efficiency of agencies involved in construction and selling of housing

Figure 5.6 Factors influencing housing supply and demand

Housing the poor

The four aspects listed at the top of this page come together in what is the greatest challenge in today's urban world: to provide decent housing for the poorer sections of urban society. Poverty creates a downward spiral so far as housing is concerned. Low income means:

- being forced to rent rather than buy
- having to put up with inadequate housing
- finding decent housing more and more inaccessible, particularly when and where housing is in short supply and costs rise.

In the North, it is largely national governments that have taken initiatives to increase the supply of low-income housing. In the South, it has been left rather more to the poor to take care of their housing needs.

Case study: Public housing in Britain

Local authority housing (or **council housing** as it is sometimes called) has been provided in Britain since 1919. It is intended to meet the housing needs of those who for various reasons (most often low income) are unable or unwilling to buy their own homes. Instead of repaying a mortgage, occupants (known as **tenants**) pay a weekly or monthly rent to the local authority.

There are three basic types of purpose-built council housing in Britain (**5.2**).

- First, there are the inter-war estates built between 1919 and 1939. These contain some of the best and also some of the worst local authority housing. Much of it is in the form of semi-detached and terraced properties.
- Secondly, there are the large council estates built between 1945 and 1965. These are more suburban in location and appearance. They are low-density developments of semi-detached two-storey housing.
- Finally, there is the post-1965 housing found mainly in inner-city areas on redeveloped sites (see page 47). Two types can be distinguished. On the one hand there are the high-rise tower blocks of the 1960s and 1970s. They proved very unpopular and were often ill-suited to the needs of the occupying households. Fortunately, they are no longer being built. On the other hand there is the high-density, low-rise housing that continues to be built today.

About 30 per cent of Britain's housing stock is made up of local authority housing. There is no doubt that much has been achieved in meeting the housing needs of lower-income households.

In the 1980s, the government introduced the 'right to buy' scheme. Sitting tenants were given the chance to buy their houses outright or by means of a mortgage. The argument was that the proceeds of the sales would allow local authorities to build more modern public housing. There are instances in London and other cities where local authorities have sold complete high-rise blocks to developers. These blocks have then been thoroughly modernised and the flats sold to owner-occupiers.

Figure 5.7 Low-income housing in Lusaka

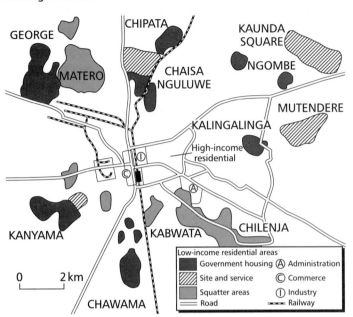

GEORGE

CHIPATA

KAUNDA SQUARE

MATERO

NGOMBE

CHAISA NGULUWE

MUTENDERE

KALINGALINGA

High-income residential

KANYAMA

KABWATA

CHILENJA

0   2 km

CHAWAMA

Low-income residential areas
- ■ Government housing ⒶAdministration
- ▨ Site and service Ⓒ Commerce
- ▦ Squatter areas Ⓘ Industry
- ═ Road ┅ Railway

Lusaka, the capital city of Zambia, has a population of just under 1 million. A significant proportion of people do not earn enough to gain access to decent housing. Much of their housing demand is met by shanty towns that have grown up on the edge of the city (**5.7**). They are illegal, but they survive mainly because they tend to occupy 'difficult' land ignored by developers. Since these are essentially spontaneous settlements, they lack the required infrastructure of water, sewerage, paved streets and electricity.

Government and city authorities recognise the need to help the really poor. They have built basic public housing that is available for rent. This is located either in run-down parts of the inner city or at the edge of the built-up area (**5.7**). A significant sector of such housing extends south-eastwards from the city centre. But funds are not available to meet in full the huge demand for low-income housing. The demand continues to rise because of high rates of rural–urban migration and natural increase.

'Site and service' schemes are an interesting attempt to improve living conditions. They have been applied to some of the older squatter areas (**5.7**). They begin with the city authorities recognising the rights of the squatters to the land they occupy. Public money is then spent on providing a basic infrastructure of water and electricity supplies, roads and drainage. In return, the squatters are expected to improve their homes by replacing the scrap building materials with bricks, mortar and proper roofing, and possibly adding properly-built new rooms.

Homelessness

Homelessness is a clear indicator that society has failed to provide for the most needy. Homeless people are the front-line victims of the imbalance between housing supply and demand. For them, it means no access to housing. The global homeless population is put at between 100 million and 1 billion – it depends how you define 'homelessness'. The lower estimate probably applies to those who have no shelter at all and who sleep outside on pavements, in doorways, in parks or under bridges. The higher estimate would include those in very insecure or temporary accommodation, much of which is of poor quality. For instance, there are **squatters** who have found accommodation by illegally occupying someone else's property or land. Their collective presence gives rise to the **shanty towns** that are to be found in so many cities in the South. They live in constant fear of eviction. Also in this category are those people living in refugee camps and hostels for the down-and-out.

Case study: Pavement dwellers in Bombay (Mumbai)

Pavement dwellers live in small shacks made of temporary materials. They utilise the walls or fences that separate building compounds from the pavement and the street outside. They can be seen in most large cities in India, but are most concentrated in Bombay and Delhi. There are estimated to be at least 250 000 such people in Bombay alone.

Most pavement dwellings are less than 5m² in extent. For this reason, the pavement in front becomes an important part of domestic space. Water is obtained from nearby housing, whilst most use public toilets for which a nominal payment has to be made.

Pavement households usually have at least one employed member. Contrary to popular belief, very few of these people make their livelihood from begging. Rather, they generally represent a pool of very cheap labour that is prepared to take on the unpleasant jobs not usually tackled by organised labour. Most work within the **informal economy** as petty traders and hawkers, cobblers and tailors, handcart pullers and wastepickers. Because they have minimal housing and travel costs, they are able to survive on very low wages.

Figure 5.8 A pavement dwelling in Bombay

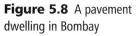

People who become pavement dwellers do so in the belief that it is only a temporary measure. The sad fact is that most never manage to make it into better housing. They live out the rest of their lives on the pavement.

Homelessness is very much an urban problem, but it would be wrong to suppose that it only occurs in LEDCs. Indeed, the proportion of people who are sleeping rough or in a night shelter may be higher in some of the world's wealthier cities. This is because such cities have a higher proportion of people who lack the income to find even the cheapest accommodation.

Case study: Homeless people in Europe and North America

Recent studies have undermined the long-held belief that the homeless tend to be older, single men.

In both Europe and North America, a growing proportion of homeless people are women – many with children. About 40 per cent of people taking advantage of services for the homeless within the European Union (EU) are women. A third of the young single homeless people arriving at the Centrepoint emergency centre in Central London are female. Single-parent households, most of which are headed by women, are particularly vulnerable. This is because the chances of finding a job, particularly if the children are too young to go to school, are very limited.

The average age of the homeless has also fallen in recent decades. In the EU, over 70 per cent of the homeless are now under the age of 40. Homeless people tend to have below-average levels of education. It is often their difficulties in finding work that makes them homeless. In Germany, 80 per cent of those in shelters have not progressed beyond primary schooling.

There is also a widespread belief that the homeless population is made up largely of people with mental illnesses and with problems of alcohol and drug abuse. Certainly, such people all too readily become homeless. Their plight is not helped by the decrease in government support services. Even so, they still form only a small proportion of the homeless.

Major causes of homelessness are job loss, a sudden fall in income, the break-up of relationships and a decline in the availability of cheap rented accommodation. Studies in Europe and North America show that the relative importance of these different underlying causes of homelessness varies considerably from country to country, from city to city.

Review

6 Of the aspects listed in **5.5**, which do you think poses the most serious health risk in Britain?

7 With reference to **5.6**, explain how each of the listed factors affects the demand or supply of housing.

8 Outline the contrasts between the North and the South when it comes to housing the urban poor.

9 How does the structure of Lusaka compare with the model described in **Chapter 4 Section E**?

10 In what ways do the urban homeless in the North differ from those in the South?

SECTION C

Keeping the city moving

Congestion and its causes

Traffic congestion is a feature of everyday city life the world over. It is so severe as to seriously threaten the well-being of many cities. The congestion arises from a number of factors:

- a growth in the number of motor vehicles
- a growth in car dependence
- the traditional concentration of activities in city centres
- a failure to make adequate provision for the motor vehicle
- a failure to come up with viable and attractive alternative modes of transport.

The rise in the number of cars worldwide in recent decades has been far more rapid than the growth in urban population. For instance, in 1950 there were around 53 million cars on the world's roads, three-quarters of them in the USA. By 1990, there were more than 400 million and another 100 million lorries, buses and commercial vehicles. Around one-third of these were in Europe, another third in North America and the final third in the rest of the world. Perhaps not surprisingly, in all world regions a large proportion of all motor vehicles is found on urban roads.

A high level of vehicle dependence was created in the North during the second half of the 20th century. Falling energy prices and rising car ownership transformed cities. They allowed:

- increased physical separation of different urban land uses
- the dispersal of employment, retailing and services from urban centres
- the creation of a low-density built-up area.

Lower densities have meant a decline in pedestrian accessibility, an extension of journey lengths and the thinning of passenger catchments. The last has been anathema to the provision of public transport. One benefit of decentralisation is that it has reduced the journey- generating potential and strength of the city centre. But much still remains there and it is a simple fact of geometry that convergence to a point spells congestion.

Most cities have spent very large sums of public money on road improvements and new roads within and around the margins of their built-up areas. However, the increased urban road capacity is immediately filled, if not exceeded, by the relentless increase in road traffic.

Solutions

Public transport has the potential to be more space-efficient and environmentally friendly than motorised private transport. Attempts to prise people out of their cars and onto public transport are constantly being made in the cities of the North. A whole of range of 'stick-and-carrot' measures have been tried, particularly to keep private cars out of city centres. Park-and-ride schemes, high car-parking charges, restricted parking, pedestrianisation and subsidised public transport fares are amongst the measures used. Users need to be persuaded that public transport can deliver a quick, reliable and competitively priced alternative. To deliver such promises clearly calls for much investment and, probably, a high level of subsidy. But where does this capital come from?

Successes in the battle against the car have been few and far apart. The reliance on public transport is quite heavy in large cities that combine severe traffic congestion and the availability of underground and surface rail networks or some other form of rapid transit. In the cores of historic cities in Europe, there are instances where public transport has gained at the expense of car travel mainly because of narrow streets and the virtual absence of parking space. Here, walking and cycling have also revived.

Case study: Containing the car in three European cities

Zurich

In the 1970s this Swiss city made a far-reaching decision about its old tram system. Instead of bowing to the car lobby and scrapping the tram system (as most European cities had done before them), the authorities decided to extend it and to upgrade services. As the revived tram service became popular with the travelling public, attention turned to providing other amenities in the central area. Pedestrian shopping malls and outdoor cafés were allowed to take over road space and parking lots. The result has been a spectacular increase in the use of public transport and a halt to the rise in car use. The key to Zurich's success is that it provided something more appealing than a car-dominated central city.

Copenhagen

This Danish city has followed a more social approach. Starting in the 1970s, the amount of car-parking space in the centre was reduced by

3 per cent each year. Each year, more central-city housing was built or refurbished. Streets were made more attractive to pedestrians and to street life in general. This involved landscaping, introducing cosmetic touches like sculptures as well as providing seating and pavement cafés. Each year there were more street musicians, markets and street festivals. As one person put it, 'The city centre became like a good party.' In short, people were tempted out of their cars. They came to appreciate that there were real benefits to be gained from leaving the car at home and using public transport instead.

Freiburg

Freiburg in Germany is another city that has shown it is possible to virtually stop the growth of car use. The interesting thing is that between 1960 and 1990, car-ownership in the city rose from 113 to 422 per 1000 inhabitants. But the use of those cars for journeys within the city has scarcely increased at all. Freiburg's success in taming the car has been brought about by a combination of three actions:

- car use has been severely restricted (a 30km/h speed limit in residential areas; expensive and limited parking)
- affordable, convenient and safe alternative forms of transport have been provided (a light rail system with buses used as feeders to it)
- urban development has been tightly regulated to ensure a compact land use pattern that is conducive to public transport, bicycling and walking.

The costs

The search for solutions to the traffic congestion problem should be driven by awareness of its costs. There are at least four.

- **Consumption of non-renewable resources** The most obvious are the fuels and lubricants derived from oil. But think of all the resources that go into the making of a motor vehicle.
- **Air pollution.**
- **Noise generation.**
- **Death and injury** Globally, road traffic accidents are thought to be the leading cause of death among adolescents and young adults.

What needs to be remembered is that all these costs also apply to public transport. To them may also be added the reduced flexibility, convenience and choice of public as opposed to private transport. Clearly, some sort of compromise or balance needs to be sought. Keeping the city moving is indeed a very real challenge. Slow-grinding traffic is a waste of non-renewable resources as well as of people's time and money.

City transport in the South

Many major cities in the South face the same problems as in the North: traffic congestion and associated air pollution. Although, in general, rates of car-ownership are lower, less road provision in cities, poor road maintenance and poorly functioning traffic management systems often mean high levels of congestion. Congestion combined with less efficient and poorly maintained engines and higher levels of lead-based additives in fuel can often mean higher levels of vehicle-related air pollution. Higher levels can be achieved even though the number of vehicles on the road is significantly less.

In many cities, the quality of public transport is poor. In recent years, it has been falling further and further behind demand. The growth in the supply of public transport is frequently slower than population growth. This supply deficit is intensified. The larger the city grows, the longer becomes the average urban journey. It is commonplace to find that a high proportion of all trips on so-called public transport are provided by informal private-sector services, ranging from rickshaws to lorries, from taxis to buses.

The spatial incoherence of the built-up area creates problems, particularly for public transport. For example, there are many areas into which buses cannot go. These include historic centres where roads and lanes are too narrow, as well as all the illegal squatter and shanty settlements. The haphazard distributions of low-income housing and places of work also make it very difficult to organise cost-effective public transport.

The impact of telecommunications technology

At the time of writing, there is no end in sight to the traffic problems that bedevil cities. People are now hoping that some sort of salvation may lie in advances in telecommunications. These developments are already transforming the way that many people work, shop, learn and communicate. They are also changing where people live and work. As a consequence, they are beginning to have an impact on urban form. Basically, the developments may be seen as reducing the need for people to travel quite so much (**5.9**).

Three aspects of the current communications or information revolution are important here. First, we need to realise that a personal computer, a modem and a telephone line in a remote rural location allow just as much connection to other users and information services that are 'on line' as the same set-up in a large city. Secondly, the speed of information transfer down telephone lines is increasing all the time. Faster modems, fibre-optic cables and digital telephone exchanges are important contributors here. Thirdly, the costs of communication are falling as the whole communications business scales up and becomes even more efficient.

These developments perhaps allow us to see the **death of distance**. Soon the need to agglomerate in towns and cities in order to achieve efficient communication and instant information exchanges will be a thing of the past. That has mighty implications for the future of towns and cities and for the future form and structure of human settlement.

Figure 5.9 Modern telecommunications will probably help to reduce traffic congestion in city centres

Review

11 To what extent is traffic congestion likely to be lessened by the decentralisation of services and jobs from city centres?

12 Compare the urban traffic problems of the North with those of the South.

13 Which of the three schemes – Zurich, Copenhagen and Freiburg – impresses you most? Give your reasons. Which type of scheme would be most likely to succeed in the UK?

14 How would you define the **telecommunications revolution**?

15 Make a list of other issues affecting city centres. Suggest and justify a ranking.

Enquiry

For a town or city that you know at first hand, investigate the provision of local authority housing. Follow up these questions:

- Are you able to recognise the types of estate described in the case study?

- How would you rate each type of area as a place in which to live?

- What was the take-up of the right-to-buy scheme?

- How much new council housing has been built in the last ten years?

TRINITY GRAMMAR SCHOOL

The city backlash – issues at the fringe and beyond

In this chapter, we look beyond the suburbs of the MEDC city. The process of **decentralisation** dominates the scene. It brings about an outward rippling of urbanisation in its broadest sense. In general, there is a gradient of declining urban influence away from the city. Some might see this as representing an urban backlash – a sort of recoil reaction of the city on the countryside.

Standing at the margin of the suburbs and looking out into countryside, it is possible to identify at least four concentric zones. Each is distinguished by a particular blend of processes, current trends and issues (**6.1**). Not all cities will replicate this simple model. For example, not all cities are constrained by green belts that seek to stop the outward spread of the built-up area. Where cities are located close together, their commuter belts may well have encroached upon and consumed what at one time was intervening rural space. In most cases, the concentric zones defined in the model will become distorted, being stretched outwards along major transport axes. Such axes are the lines of least resistance to the spread of urban influences.

Before taking a look at each of these four belts, we need to be clear about the make-up of the decentralisation process and the ways in which urban influences are carried beyond the edge of the town or city.

Figure 6.1
Decentralisation and the four belts beyond the city

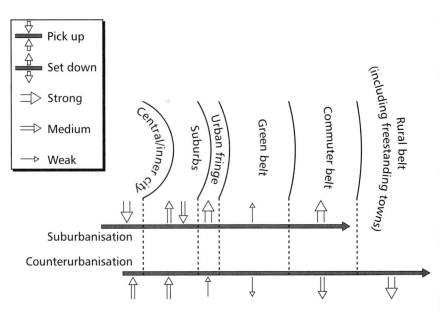

Processes in tandem

Decentralisation in the context of the urban world refers to the outward movement of people, jobs and services from central-city and inner-city areas to the suburbs and from there progressively deeper out into the countryside. The outward movement in fact involves two fairly distinct processes. They differ in terms of their start and finish points, as well as distances involved and the nature of the environment at the destination. The processes are suburbanisation and counterurbanisation. It might be helpful to think of these two processes as transit systems (**6.1**).

Suburbanisation picks up 'passengers' in the city centre and inner city. Many are dropped off in the suburbs and the urban fringe but others carry on across the green belt and are set down in the commuter belt. Normal services end there. **Counterurbanisation**, on the other hand, picks up 'passengers' in all three city zones, particularly the suburbs. Stops are rarely made in the urban fringe, but setting down begins weakly in the green belt and strengthens across the commuter belt. The bulk of 'passengers' are set down in the rural belt, major stops being in villages and small towns. So suburbanisation generally involves shorter 'journeys'; its destinations may be described as being typically 'low-density urban with a hint of rurality'. In contrast, the destinations of counterurbanisation may be more overtly rural, but also involve urban settlements that are usually smaller than the original town or city.

Perhaps it would help now to consolidate matters with some definitions. **Counterurbanisation** is a process leading to a redistribution of population and some employment. In this, large cities decline (or stagnate) in population due to net migration losses, while villages and small- to medium-sized free-standing towns gain in size because of net migration gains. It is therefore a process of deconcentration or decentralisation. It is not a complete reversal of urbanisation, because it perpetuates some of the same trends. For example, it too involves people moving out of agriculture and into manufacturing and service jobs. For this reason, counterurbanisation is sometimes referred to as **decentralised urbanisation**. By it, urbanisation in the broadest sense is being more widely diffused. **Suburbanisation** also involves a redistribution, but not just of people. The process is one that brings about the extension of the city's built-up area. As we shall see later, these extensions are not always contiguous. Suburbanisation is a much older process than counterurbanisation.

Review

1 Compare **suburbanisation** and **counterurbanisation** by making a list of their differences and similarities.

2 Make a revised and annotated version of **6.1** to create a model of those situations where there is no formal green belt.

The urban fringe

Our examination of the impact of the two decentralisation processes starts in the suburbs at the very edge of the built-up area (**6.1**). In **Chapter 4 Section A** we highlighted the dynamism of this part of the city. High levels of growth are being experienced because of the influx, not just of people but also of retailing, offices and industries. This is the number one beneficiary of the decentralisation that dominated urbanisation in the North throughout much of the 20th century. Beyond the consolidated and established suburbs, there is a zone of transition in which bricks and mortar give way to green space. In many parts of the world, the transition is a slow and gradual one, giving rise to quite a wide fringe belt. However, in the UK and other MEDCs planning intervention has sought to make the belt a narrow one. In landscape terms, the break between town and country is intended to be quite a clean one.

Case study: Meadowhall, Sheffield

Figure 6.2 Aerial view of Meadowhall

Meadowhall is a huge retailing complex located on the north-eastern outskirts of Sheffield close to Junction 34 on the M1 motorway. On its two levels it accommodates over 100 shops. Amongst these is an impressive number of flagship stores. These include Marks & Spencer, C & A, House of Fraser, Debenhams, Boots, W H Smith, and a huge Savacentre (a Sainsbury's hypermarket). All shops front onto covered malls and are contained within a single overarching building (Meadowhall). Other services provided in the same building are some 30 restaurants, cafés and bars, and a crèche.

Although this greenfield development was planned on the basis that the majority of shoppers would travel by car (there is a huge provision of parking places, together with two Savacentre petrol stations), it is served by a passenger transport interchange. This is capable of handling 120 buses each hour; it also includes two railway stations, and is served by Sheffield's own 'supertram'.

Clearly, the customer catchment of Meadowhall is expected to be far greater than just Sheffield and its immediate environs. Easily within a 45-minute travel-time are Barnsley, Chesterfield, Derby, Doncaster, Huddersfield, Leeds, Mansfield, Nottingham and Worksop. This isoline contains a potential market of well over 2 million customers.

What has yet to be established is the impact of the opening of Meadowhall on retailing in central Sheffield and in those towns and cities located within the 45-minute isoline. Another issue concerns the use of a largely greenfield site for this huge development when Sheffield has a sizeable stock of brownfield sites within its borders.

The major issue here is one of space allocation. Given the dynamism of the suburbs and the urban fringe, there is a huge and apparently insatiable demand for **greenfield** or undeveloped space, particularly for sites close to motorways and main roads. The key question is whether this demand should be controlled or managed in any way? Or should these fringe activities be allowed to invade this accessible rural space at will?

Review

3 Make a list of the costs and benefits of compressing the urban fringe.

In the UK throughout the second half of the 20th century there was a concern about the erosion of rural space by urban growth. The original argument was that Britain badly needs its farmland. However, in an age of food surpluses, the argument changed rather to conserving the countryside for nature and for leisure amenities. Although the arguments may have changed, Britain has consistently pursued policies that constrain suburban growth and the outward push of the urban fringe.

SECTION C

The green belt

All of Britain's conurbations and most of its sizeable cities are encircled by green belts. Most green belts were designated in the early post-war period. They were central to the **urban containment strategy**. The aim was quite simply to prevent urban sprawl from rampaging unchecked into the countryside. The aim was also to make the urban fringe much crisper and more clearly defined. The belts vary in width from a few kilometres to over 15. In England, green belts now account for 12 per cent of the land area. In general, they have been quite successful in achieving their basic aim, but unsuspected costs have also been incurred. In trying to evaluate this planning device which has made its mark on the British landscape, it is necessary to examine its impact on three different spatial locations – on areas inside, within and outside the green belt.

Inside the green belt

Inside the green belt, the amount of land available for new urban growth immediately became fixed. The built-up area could now only fill up those vacant spaces that happened to exist at the time when the green belt was designated. This created an unfortunate set of consequences. Because land for development became a scarce resource, its price shot up. This in turn significantly raised housing costs and also residential densities. By building at higher densities, the site-cost element in the price of a dwelling could be kept to an acceptable level. But the rationing of land also encouraged cutting back on the amount of space that could be set aside for those amenities and services that are required by a modern residential community. Schools, shops, playing fields and parks were just some of the things that suffered.

So the green belt may have been good in terms of firming up the edge of the city and preventing suburban sprawl. At the same time, however, it made the suburbs more urban by raising housing densities and pruning the amount of green space. Worst of all, for so many people, it meant smaller dwellings and higher housing costs. But at least they were now within easy reach, if not sight, of open countryside.

Within the green belt

Within the green belt itself, the main aim was to protect and conserve the countryside and its associated settlements. Development pressures were to be resisted almost at all costs. This was mixed news for farmers. Their agricultural future was assured, but they could no longer reap huge profits from selling land to developers. One unsuspected backlash has been the social up-grading of many settlements within the green belt. Because of the protection afforded to villages and hamlets, housing within them has become a desirable commodity. This was particularly so for more affluent people wishing to combine an urban job with a rural life-style. As house prices rocketed, so many of those employed in farming and other local jobs were gradually squeezed out of the green belt housing market.

Over the years, there has been a slight easing of green belts. This has been in response to two pressures. First, because many green belts were too tightly drawn originally, growth pressures on the inside built up to an intolerable level. There had to be some reduction of these pressures. Secondly, there have been pressures to make a wider use of the green belt and its resources, particularly to meet the needs of the nearby city. No longer was it viable to keep the green belt just for the farmers. There are now a number of permitted uses. These include providing recreational facilities, from golf courses to football pitches, caravan parks to riding stables. Sand and gravel working is another example, but with strict regulations about either restoring sites to their original use or turning water-filled areas into nature reserves and fishing lakes. Land can also be released for public utilities, such as reservoirs, sewage treatment works and rubbish incinerators.

This last permitted land use leads us easily into considering one of the possible downsides of the green belt as a protected area. All cities make an **ecological footprint**. Most obvious is the destruction of natural habitats to make way for the built-up area. Diagram **6.3** reminds us that there are others, but the significance of most of these is that they are not only felt within the polluter city. Rural areas immediately around the city – and that includes the green belt – suffer too. Rivers and streams flowing through the city are likely to be contaminated by discharges from factories and so pass the effluent out into the countryside. Areas on the leeward side of the city will certainly share some

Figure 6.3 The city as an ecological system

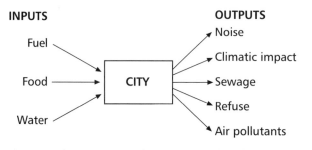

of its atmospheric pollution. Green belt space will also be called upon to help the city in related ways, as for example in connection with urban water supply, sewage treatment and refuse disposal (see *The Fragile Environment* in the EPICS series).

Case study: The environmental impact of the M25

Building the M25 motorway in the green belt was perhaps inevitable given the need:

- to build some sort of mega-bypass around London
- to avoid destroying any of London's built-up area
- to put some green space between it and the suburban edge
- to catch most of the circulating traffic reasonably close to London.

In the event, the routeing of the motorway took it far enough away from the suburban edge to ensure that residents were not too affected by noise or fumes (**6.4**). Instead those environmental costs are borne mainly by the farming community and those more affluent people living in the green belt.

Some would argue that the full economic benefits of the motorway are not being realised. This arises because green belt status precludes almost all forms of development. But think of the various activities that would relish and benefit from a site along this motorway. The case for releasing land on the London side of the motorway seems to be a compelling one.

The case of the M25 illustrates a recurring conflict of interests. On the one hand, there are the economic development pressures and the need to maximise the benefits of a major investment in infrastructure. Set against these is the long-standing government commitment to protect agricultural land and the environment.

Figure 6.4 Environmental impact of the M25

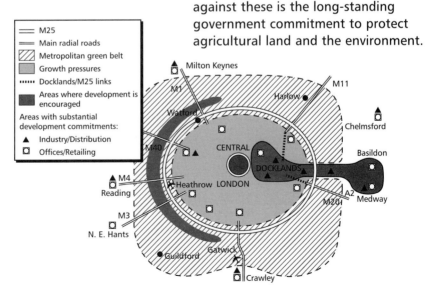

Key:
= M25
= Main radial roads
▨ Metropolitan green belt
▦ Growth pressures
••••• Docklands/M25 links
▬ Areas where development is encouraged
Areas with substantial development commitments:
▲ Industry/Distribution
◻ Offices/Retailing

Figure 6.5 Extract from *The Times*, 2 January 1999

Case study: The green belt under threat

CAMBRIDGE

Donald Douglas, a *Times* reader, is concerned about green belt land in Cambridge and says areas around Addenbrookes, Trumpington and Grantchester Meadows are proposed for development. 'The green belt was set up to stop Cambridge turning into an industrial town,' he says. 'It has worked for the past 50 years and we need it now more than ever under the threat of housing development.' According to Brian Human, from Cambridge City Council: 'The use of green belt land is the most effective way of accommodating the growth coming to Cambridge.' He denies that any specific areas have been marked out for release but emphasised that a review of green belt boundaries was imperative.

The recent study conducted by the council argues that 'some parts of the green belt could, if developed sensitively, make a vital contribution to nurturing the social and economic wellbeing of the city'. It says the existence of the green belt has driven up house prices in Cambridge and encouraged commuting by car into the city centre. A Conservative spokesman on the Environment Committee says that improved public transport and development of the city centre would in fact eliminate the need to destroy the green belt.

STEVENAGE

Juliet Pennington, a *Times* reader from Hertfordshire, is angered by the Government's go-ahead for plans to build 10,000 homes on green belt land between Hitchin and Stevenage. 'I would be dismayed to see such a huge chunk of farmland covered by houses,' she says. An action group, Campaign Against Stevenage Expansion (CASE), has been established to campaign against this development. Jenny Purchon, from CASE, argues that the housing estate could be built on nearby brownfield sites rather than on this 'totally rural and pleasant countryside'.

Stevenage was part of the second wave of postwar new towns and its green belt was integral to its design. It forms part of the Greater London belt and was extended in 1986. Proposals in the Hertfordshire County Structure Plan to build 3,600 houses by 2011 – with a view to develop up to 10,000 more in the long term – were approved by the Secretary of State in April 1998. Rob Shipway, key housing sites manager at Hertfordshire County Council, explains: 'This level of development simply cannot be accommodated on brownfield sites alone. We have to look at the most sustainable option which in this case is to utilise green belt land.'

DERBYSHIRE

Stuart Hutchby writes from Derbyshire where about 32 hectares of green belt land in Draycott and Breaston have been acquired by Westermans, the developer, as a site for up to 1,000 houses. Derbyshire County Council and Erewash Borough Council have opposed the plans but Hutchby believes their opposition 'would have little sway if this is taken further'. Derbyshire County Council's recent structure plan found little need for extra housing, but developers have tabled objections and the plan faces a public inquiry. David Staples, senior planning officer at Erewash Borough Council, emphasises that the council 'wants to accommodate growth within the unprotected areas of the borough'; 85 per cent of Erewash Borough is green belt which the council wants to keep 'largely intact'. Christine Barker, of South Derbyshire CPRE, is concerned that the public inquiry could open the gates to development across the county. 'If they can get permission to alter the extent of the green belt then we fear there could be a housing free-for-all,' she explains. The green belt between Derby and Nottingham was established in 1982 to check urban sprawl and keep the two cities separate, but has come under threat from speculative purchases by local builders.

Britain's green belts are now under even more severe pressure. County and local authorities in England accept that it is necessary to build over 4 million new homes in the next ten years or so. The question is: where to build? On greenfield sites in the countryside seems to be the answer rather than on brownfield sites (see **Case study, Chapter 4 Section B**). Where better than on farmland in the green belt! Already something like 4000ha of green belt land has been released to the developers. The case study above (**6.5**) gives some detail of specific threats in the views of three people. They are all on the same side in the issue.

Beyond the green belt

The third spatial aspect of the green belt takes us to the next ring, the commuter belt (**6.1**). To round off this section, all that is needed is to make one point. The green belt's main impact has been to push the commuter belt further out into the countryside. It has lengthened the average daily commuter journey by twice its width – that is, the commuter is forced to cross the green belt twice in a day. Longer journeys mean higher travel costs. Commuters are obliged to pay in time and money for the privilege of passing through what is in effect a no-go area (that is, to all but the most affluent workers).

Review

4 Identify the main components of Britain's urban containment policy.

5 Give an explanation for the social upgrading that has occurred in green belt settlements.

6 Explain and illustrate what is meant by the **ecological footprint of a city**.

7 With reference to the M25 case study, identify the sorts of activity that would benefit from a motorway location.

8 With reference to the M25 case study, state where you stand on the issue of economic pressures versus protection of the countryside. State your arguments.

9 Put together a case to support the use of green belt for new housing.

SECTION D

The commuter belt

Dormitory developments

Much of the decentralisation to this belt takes the form of suburban development (**6.1**). Because of the green belt, the suburbs are detached from the mother city and wrapped instead around outlying villages and small towns to create so-called **dormitory settlements**. Many of the working residents of the new estates are commuters. They are people who in a sense want a foot in both camps. They want to be near a city because of its better job opportunities and higher salary levels. They are also keen to take advantage of the higher-order services that a city offers. On the other hand, the dormitory settlement offers relatively cheaper housing, more space and a pseudo-rural environment. The price that has to be paid for seeking the best of two worlds is the actual commuting. Commuting has its physical and monetary costs; it also needs a daily investment of time. The suburbanisation of settlements in the commuter belt tends to be greatest where access to the city is best. That means along railways, motorways and main roads. In these, the scale of the suburbanisation can be so great as to completely obliterate the original character of settlements.

In the sectors between the main transport routes, commuter developments may be a little more up-market. Farmhouses are converted into spacious and expensive properties and fields used as paddocks for the grazing of ponies and horses. It is also still possible within these sectors to come across areas beyond the reach of even the most hardy commuter. Here perhaps former farm workers' cottages are bought up as second homes or taken over by couples making a retirement move out of the city. Such changes seem to be more a part of counterurbanisation than suburbanisation.

Overspill

In Britain, the commuter belt also contains **new towns** (such as Harlow and Crawley) and **expanded towns** (such as Basingstoke and Aylesbury) that were part of the post-war **overspill** programme (see **Case study, Chapter 3 Section B**). In this programme, the planners tried to slim down the conurbations and major cities by persuading people and jobs to shift out of them. The important difference with these overspill schemes, as compared with the dormitory settlements, was that the people moving to them would find work locally and not commute back to the city. Although they have all become important employment centres, long-distance commuters have also moved in.

Case study: The decentralisation of factories and offices in South East England

Restricting the growth of employment in London became another weapon in the British urban containment strategy. It was felt that expansion of the industrial sector and later the office sector was generating too much growth within the conurbation. Thus legislation was introduced that restricted the expansion of firms and the setting up of new ones in Central and Inner London. At the same time, incentives were offered to persuade firms to move out of the conurbation altogether rather than just shift to the suburbs.

The maps **6.6** and **6.7** show that most of the overspill moves were destined for the Outer Metropolitan Area beyond the green belt. Virtually all ended up in either well-established towns or new towns. This

Figure 6.6 The movement of industry in South East England

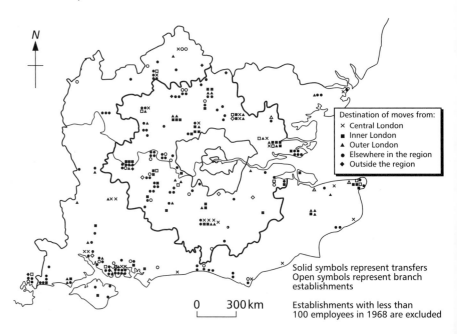

Destination of moves from:
× Central London
■ Inner London
▲ Outer London
● Elsewhere in the region
◆ Outside the region

Solid symbols represent transfers
Open symbols represent branch establishments

0   300 km

Establishments with less than 100 employees in 1968 are excluded

Figure 6.7 Office moves in South East England

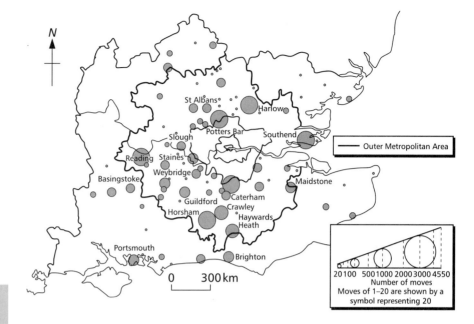

- Outer Metropolitan Area

St Albans · Harlow · Potters Bar · Slough · Southend · Reading · Staines · Weybridge · Basingstoke · Maidstone · Guildford · Caterham · Horsham · Crawley · Haywards Heath · Portsmouth · Brighton

N

0   300 km

20 100 500 1000 2000 3000 4550
Number of moves
Moves of 1–20 are shown by a
symbol representing 20

Review

10 Make an analysis of the origins of the industrial moves shown in **6.6**.

11 Explain why the planned decentral-isation of jobs from London gave the destination towns the chance to become free-standing.

12 What is your opinion of the changes taking place in the commuter belt? Are they part of suburb-anisation or coun-terurbanisation? Justify your view.

considerable shift of jobs not only helped to slim down London, but clearly boosted urban growth in the commuter belt. The decentralisation gave these towns the chance to become free-standing rather than London satellites.

Suburbanisation or counterurbanisation?

Given the situation in this belt of suburbanised settlements separated by rural space, it would be fair to claim that this is truly the **rural–urban fringe**. Much of that rural space is still being farmed, but equally it is increasingly used for recreation. It may be for informal use, such as country walks and bird watching, or it may be for recreation of a more formal kind like golf and horse-riding. Are the processes at work here suburbanisation or counterurbanisation? The environments created certainly have a suburban feel about them. However, the growth of dormitory settlements only takes place because people are in a sense reacting against life in the big city. Their preference is for a less intensively urban way of life. They are happy to put space between their homes and the big city. Planned overspill certainly qualifies as counterurbanisation because it involves the movement of growth down the urban hierarchy. So too do any retirement moves originating in the city.

SECTION E

The rural belt

In this final belt, we look beyond the rural–urban fringe to areas that on a number of counts should be classified as rural (**6.1**). But even in these remoter areas – perhaps well over an hour's travel-time from a city – it is difficult to escape completely from the urban world. Certainly, pollution can be quite noticeable here downstream and downwind of a major city, particularly if it is a centre of heavy manufacturing. The belt will contain settlements of a market-town type. It will certainly be visited by urban people for a range of purposes. On this basis, it is perhaps possible to recognise three types of rural space.

Amenity areas

Generally, these are parts of the belt that have something to offer urban folk in the contexts of leisure and recreation. They may fall within Areas of Outstanding Natural Beauty or National Parks. They attract urban people either as day-trippers or as weekend and weekly tourists. Their attractions may include such things as fine scenery, walking and climbing opportunities or lakes and rivers for a whole range of water-based sports. It may well be that cottages are bought up by affluent urban dwellers as second homes for use at weekends and during holidays. Perhaps the greatest impact will be caused by a variety of commercial activities that seek to take advantage of the attractions, for example:

- large houses converted into hotels
- farmhouses offering bed-and-breakfast
- souvenir and craft shops
- 'cream tea' cafés.

The good news for such areas is that these manifestations of the tourist industry provide employment and income to supplement that from the traditional rural activities such as farming and forestry.

Accessible areas

These could include amenity areas, but the key feature is their accessibility from one or more major cities. They have proved particularly attractive to firms wishing to set up branch factories or branch offices. The locations chosen are usually small towns and this point serves to make a timely reminder. It is important to remember that despite the prevalence of rural space, this belt as a whole is not without its small- to medium-sized towns. Most will have originated as market towns and in general they are widely spaced.

The accessible areas are also exploited by long-distance (weekly rather than daily) commuters and second-home buyers. These incomers will also include those who have decided to drop out of the urban rat-race altogether and settle for a quieter and less stressful life-style. These are the true counterurbanites – perhaps we might call them the **urban dropouts**. Rural settlements begin to change as the number of these incomers increases. Their arrival certainly stimulates the property market, and prices begin to rise. This in turn could rebound on local households who find themselves gradually priced out of the more attractive housing.

Figure 6.8 Extract from *The Times*, 16 December 1998

Case study: The loss of village shops

A closed chapter in village history

Five or six village shops close each week, says the Village Retail Services Association (ViRSA). Among recent casualties are Jean and Barry Frampton, who are about to shut up shop for the last time. The couple have been running Mereworth Stores, in the village of Mereworth, Kent, for the past 27 years but have decided to sell up and retire. Trade is dropping off and they are unable to compete with the big boys.

Almost 3,000 out of 11,000 villages are now without a shop. ViRSA cites a 15 to 20 per cent decline in the number of single stores, in villages with populations of 1,000 or fewer, over the past ten years, which means that five or six such shops are closing each week.

Any reversal in the trend, says the Association, will depend on the future effects of transport policy, incentives to increase trade, and education of the rural population to support their community generally.

Mrs Frampton says: 'Trade has dropped in the past three years and we never see some villagers. We used to get quite a bit of passing trade, people going to and from work, but they can pull up at the petrol stations to buy milk, cigarettes and so on. We still have many regulars but no one does a big shop in the village stores as they did when we started out 27 years ago.'

Times are changing, as David Parry at Cluttons Daniel Smith in Maidstone, which is handling the sale, is aware: 'At the moment, the closing of a village shop seems to be an economic fact of life. It is always a sad event when it happens and quite difficult, not only for the vendors, who have invariably run the business all of their working lives, but for the community as well.

'They are faced with living in a place that no longer has the amenities it once had. Similarly, it begins to erode our perception of village life – a community that centres on the church, school and village shop.'

Kent lost another village shop this summer, in Mersham. It closed at the end of August after 150 years of trading. Countess Mountbatten of Burma was one of many residents upset at the loss. She emphasised the importance of the local shop in village life: 'I shop there regularly and my in-laws, who have lived in the village for years, also shop there. It's the most awful tragedy for the village.

'The thing is, it is not just the village store, it is also a post office and a sort of mini-community centre. People meet there when they are doing their shopping and exchange information. Particularly for old people who don't have a car, it is awful news.'

Changes are also afoot in the Cotswold village of Painswick, where four shops are on the market. Diane Mearns at Hamptons International in Painswick is selling the bakery and the Antiques and Craft Centre, along with Bell Cottage, a converted florists and gift shop. Such properties are being converted to residential use, or offices.

Many shopkeepers are looking to sell up, and are being advised by their estate agents to obtain planning permission for their shops to be converted into private houses before putting them on the market, to make them easier to sell.

Remote areas

Finally, there are those areas which by virtue of distance and terrain remain remote from urban centres. These are truly peripheral and disadvantaged areas which suffer from a persistent loss of population. The long-established emigration of younger people to towns and cities has recreated an irreversible **downward spiral**. What we find here are declining villages and abandoned farms. Here the issue is the apparently simple one: should these areas, the long-term victims of urbanisation, be allowed to decline into oblivion, or should some attempt be made to revive them?

In the rural belt, then, the processes of urbanisation and counter-urbanisation can be seen working almost alongside each other, but pulling in opposite directions. The negative impact of the former is seen in the loss of population, services and jobs from the really remote areas. Another is the long-distance dispersal of urban pollution. Its positive impact is to be seen in the growth of a tourist industry that is geared to a largely urban and increasingly mobile and affluent market. By comparison, the evidence of counterurbanisation varies in strength, being strongest in the accessible areas and weakest in the remote ones. Let us look a little more closely at this process.

Review

13 How valid do you think it is to distinguish the three different areas within the rural belt? Are there any other types that might be recognised?

14 Sketch what you would see as the downward spiral of decline in remote rural areas.

Counterurbanisation – character, benefits and costs

Character

Out in the rural belt, counterurbanisation involves an inward movement of:

- branch plants and branch offices, mainly to small towns
- self-employed people, often linked to the service sector
- people at or near retirement
- second homers and weekenders
- the urban dropouts.

They are moving into areas that have a prevailing air of decline, in farming, housing, population and services.

Benefits

Without doubt, counterurbanisation can bring a diversity of benefits to a range of different interest groups.

- Employers moving to the small towns reap the benefits of a reliable and manageable labour force, a lack of restrictive practices and the possibility of occupying a modern, relatively cheap, purpose-built plant in pleasant and spacious surroundings.
- The arrival of new jobs in small factories, offices and even shops creates work opportunities for local people, particularly women and redundant farmworkers.
- Inward migrants can trade off lower wages against much lower housing costs. They do not have to forgo completely the material advantages of urban living.
- Landowners can profit from the sale of land for new housing and from the sale of renovated old farm buildings.
- The arrival of relatively affluent people can encourage the selective revival of commercial (restaurants, pubs, etc.) and social (schools, medical centres, etc.) services.
- Self-employed people and their businesses, from restaurateurs to garage-owners, from guest-houses to riding stables, benefit from the influx of weekenders and tourists.
- Retired people see the drawbacks of rural living (such as limited services) more than compensated by the lower cost of living, the slower pace of life and less stress, noise and nuisance.
- The old social order controlled by the Church and aristocracy begins to break down.

With so many standing to benefit and prosper, a new community spirit emerges.

Costs

But not all is sweetness and light. Counterurbanisation does have its downside.

- Low-income local people become more disadvantaged. For example, they are squeezed by rising house prices. Public transport services deteriorate because most of the incomers have private cars. The affluence of the incomers also means that private social services (schools, medical and dental practices) flourish while public provision continues to decline.
- Retired people begin to suffer when they lose their mobility. Access to the services of old age becomes much more difficult.
- Owners of small businesses and the self-employed initially enjoy quite rich pickings. The outlook is altered, however, as new competitors are drawn to the area by the perceived opportunities.
- For some, the rural utopia becomes scarred by what they see as the urbanisation of the countryside.

- The arrival of branch businesses, and the acceptance of regional aid as part of a programme for the revival of peripheral areas, means that there is increased external control.

At the individual level, it is a matter of weighing up the costs and benefits. The population evidence is that many think counterurbanisation has brought about a change for the better. Nonetheless, there is evidence of a small return flow back to the city. For some people, there is a degree of disillusionment and dissatisfaction with the new life in the rural belt. How do we classify such people? Are they urbanites returning to the fold, or are they counter-counterurbanites?

Review

15 Why do you think that branch plants and offices are setting up in the rural belt? Why should they choose town locations?

16 What is your own assessment of the costs and benefits of counterurbanisation? If you are not there already, would you be persuaded to move to the rural belt?

SECTION G

A view from the South

Because most LEDCs are still going through the earlier stages of the urbanisation curve (see **1.2**), the patterns of movement are still mainly rural to urban. The processes are centripetal rather than centrifugal. Here, urbanisation is really causing two major problems:

- rapid and ill-planned accretion in the urban fringe belt
- persistent depopulation in rural areas.

As for the former, there are no green belts or other forms of legislation to check the tendency for the urban margins to sprawl into the countryside. The latter is still occurring on a massive scale in many countries. Undertaking day trips into rural areas for recreation is not yet really part of Third World urbanism. But even if it was, the transport situation would hardly be encouraging.

Review

17 Can you think of any other ways in which urban trends in the South differ from those in the North?

1 With reference to the case study about the closure of village shops on page 85, write a report which contains the following headings:
- The causes of village shop closures
- The social costs of closures
- Alternative types of retailing
- Alternative uses for redundant shops
- The way ahead.

2 The population of the Greater London conurbation stood at 8.3 million in 1951. Today it is just under 7 million. For this enquiry you need to examine a number of factors that have contributed to this loss of population. They are:
- Planned overspill schemes such as new towns (Harlow, Stevenage, etc.) and expanded towns (Basingstoke, Aylesbury, etc.)
- The regeneration of areas of older housing
- Decline in the rates of natural increase and in-migration
- Improvements in public and private transport
- The high cost of living
- The onset of counterurbanisation.

In your report, you should:
a explain the link between each of these factors and the decline in London's population
b identify other possible factors
c establish any links between those factors
d suggest and justify which factors have had the greatest impact.

The urban outlook

SECTION A

Sustainable urban development

Writing at this time (1999) and looking to the new millennium, one thing is certain. The global level of urbanisation will continue to rise. Many countries in the South will, at varying rates, progress along the urbanisation curve (**1.2**). In the North, whilst the level of urbanisation is unlikely to increase except in a handful of countries, the dominant process will be one of decentralisation. The trickle of growth down through the urban hierarchy may be expected to continue. Smaller towns and cities will gain from the jobs and people shed by the largest cities.

In many respects there is little that governments, North or South, can do to resist these processes. However, all governments do have a responsibility to show vision – that is, to set aims and objectives which together underlie an urban future that promises maximum benefits and minimum costs for the greatest number. The key word in all this is **sustainability** (**7.1**).

Meeting the needs of the present...	...without compromising the ability of future generations to meet their own needs
Economic needs – an adequate and secure livelihood.	Minimise the use or waste of non-renewable natural resources – reduce, use, re-use, recycle, reclaim.
Health needs – properly serviced housing; medical support for all who need it; protection from hazards and pollution.	Conserve non-renewable heritage – cultural, historical and natural assets.
Social and cultural needs – access to education; the chance to realise personal potential; equal opportunities.	Sustainable use of renewable resources, especially water, soil, wood and biomass fuels.
Political needs – freedom to participate in politics and in decision-making concerning home and the local neighbourhood.	Keep city wastes within the absorptive capacity of local (rivers) and global (oceans) sinks; create non-renewable sinks for the disposal of chemicals and pesticides.

Figure 7.1 The multiple goals of sustainable urban development

The essence of **sustainability** is carried in the sentence that heads table **7.1**. With sustainable urban development there is an even tighter focus on the environment and resources. Minimising negative impacts on the natural environment is certainly one major goal. Another is eliminating the wasteful use of non-renewable resources and using renewable resources more carefully. What we have to recognise is that

Review

1 In your own words, explain what you understand by the term **sustainable urban development**.

2 Suggest possible ways of assessing **sustainability**.

3 Can you see any significant omissions from **7.1**?

towns and cities are major players in the present environmental crisis. This arises because they are:

- major consumers of non-renewable resources and
- major producers of pollution and waste (**6.3**).

So far as environment is concerned, the challenge is to make urbanisation more 'benign'. But the environment is only one aspect of sustainability. There are economic, social, cultural and political aspects. These appear as 'needs' in **7.1**. All of them, and possibly others, are united by the need to achieve one thing: equality. So here, sustainable urban development is one that reduces disparity and injustice and maximises well-being and opportunity for all. These are fine words, but can the aims that they convey ever be achieved, and how? What does all this hold for the urban future?

Any discussion of the possible character of the urban world in the 21st century has to focus on a number of key issues.

SECTION B

The development pathway

The course of the development pathway will be a critical factor. Its twists, turns and changing surface may be expected to have a direct impact on future urbanisation, particularly its distribution and spatial patterns. First, let us take a global view and then look separately at the two main global divisions.

Globalisation

Despite the shocks to the global economy in the late 1990s, **globalisation** looks set to continue. National economies will become even more knitted together by a complex web of economic and political links. The world's leading cities (the so-called **global cities**) will consolidate their status as important nodes in this web, particularly as providers of financial and producer services. The impressive central areas of these cities and their overall extent will symbolise their immense status, power and wealth. However, urbanisation generated by globalisation does and will continue to have its downside, particularly so far as sustainability is concerned.

- Because of their scale, global cities are heavy consumers of resources and large producers of pollution.
- For all their strength and status, global cities are vulnerable, particularly to the instability of the world's financial system. Recent events such as stock market crashes, bank collapses and massive international fraud have had crippling effects on financial centres as far apart as London and Tokyo.
- In their national contexts, global cities create huge degrees of disparity and inequality. This is inevitable because each represents a massive polarisation of investment and employment. They are truly primate cities.

- Globalisation has created a new division – the 'fast world' and the 'slow world'. The former comprises the more dynamic parts of the North, whilst the latter includes most of the South as well as the North's declining regions. Whilst cities in the former are able to establish themselves as key points in the world's economic network, cities in the latter become increasingly remote from its opportunities.

So whilst continuing globalisation will provide the fuel for quite spectacular urban growth, it hardly promises a sustainable future. The success of an elite of cities inevitably creates a wake of second-class cities. At a range of spatial scales, globalisation seems set to produce inequality and environmental damage.

In the North

Two trends already apparent at the end of the 20th century will continue to make their mark on the urban world of the North. Further de-industrialisation matched by growth in the service sector is one trend. This will continue to alter the urban economic base. The second is the further hotting-up of competition between towns and cities. This comes about because of the prevalence of a market-led type of urbanisation. It is also encouraged by new technologies which allow cities to operate more efficiently both within themselves and over tributary areas.

In general, the strongest competitors have already become the leading cities. The outlook for the new millennium is that with a further strengthening of inter-city competition, more efforts will have to be made by all but the strongest to compete and survive. This will encourage more intervention by city managers, and will probably take the form of programmes aimed at boosting such things as economic growth, urban regeneration and image promotion. Such action programmes are often large consumers of resources, and rely heavily on public funds. All too often they can result in:

- reduced public spending on welfare and education
- local authority long-term debt
- the wastage of resources
- risks being taken with the environment.

Success cannot be guaranteed. There will always be the fear of diminishing returns from the investments made. In short, the competition scenario is hardly one that will create a future which is sustainable environmentally, economically or socially.

In the South

The urban future seems even more uncertain here. In theory, the de-industrialisation of the North should create opportunities for the South. But there is little security in manufacturing these days as transnational companies are forever in search of new least-cost locations for their operations. 'Here today and gone tomorrow' is an appropriate slogan.

Given the low level of consumer demand, the outlook for the service sector is not much better. In the circumstances, the informal economy may be expected to play a crucial part in holding cities back from the brink of even greater chaos and despair.

Perhaps even more worrying is the strong likelihood that rural–urban migration will continue unabated. If today's cities do not have the economic base adequately to support their present population, what hope is there in the future? The prospect must be one of continuing, perhaps deepening, inequality and poverty.

Review

4 Remind yourself of what is meant by **globalisation**.

5 Compare the likely urban futures of the North and the South.

The telecommunications revolution

There can be no doubting that advances in telecommunications will have a major impact on the future character of the urban world. Three rather different and contradictory scenarios may be anticipated.

The electronic city

Developments in telecommunications have already begun to affect the spatial pattern of urbanisation. Further decentralisation of activities such as shops, offices and shops away from city centres is one trend that can be expected to continue. This dispersion of employment to the suburbs, the rural–urban fringe and even beyond, combined with the growth of telecommuting, will certainly bring important changes:

- the volume of traffic into and out of city centres will be reduced
- there will be more flexibility in the timing of journeys-to-work
- this, in turn, may well reduce the rush-hour strain on urban transport networks.

At the same time, the application of new telecommunications technology could lead to a better monitoring and management of traffic flows.

Offsetting these potential gains is the likelihood that telecommunications facilities will become concentrated in a few leading cities. This repeats a point made earlier in connection with globalisation. Undoubtedly, these select cities will benefit as they become important nodes in the electronic economy. In short, progress in telecommunications is likely to increase economic and social inequalities within the urban system. We might anticipate the creation of **electronic ghettos** peopled by an 'information underclass'.

The edge city

The process underlying this scenario is the one already under way – decentralisation. One of its products is the **edge cities** that are mushrooming in North America. As we saw in **Chapter 4 Section A**, these are city-like settlements on the fringes of existing cities. In the opinion of some, this spatial pattern offers an environmentally sustainable and efficient form of urban development. For example, the pattern brings with it a decrease in commuting distances. However, the pattern may prove to be unsustainable socially. Experience in the USA has indicated that edge cities have a strong tendency to become socially exclusive. The heavy involvement of private developers has resulted in expensive housing, up-market services and little provision for less affluent social groups. At the same time, edge cities create another unwanted backlash as more affluent people move to them, so they leave behind downgraded and even abandoned urban areas.

The dispersed city

In an earlier chapter reference was made to the death of distance that comes in the wake of modern telecommunications. To put it baldly, the death of distance means that it is no longer necessary for people, jobs and services to agglomerate at particular points – that is, in towns and cities. There is no reason why the city as we know it should not be blown apart. A truly dispersed city would allow a more intimate juxtaposition of town and country. After all, that is why suburbs were born in the first place. That is why counterurbanisation is gathering momentum: people want the best of both worlds. A completely dispersed city would deliver just that – but think of the environmental costs!

Review

6 Create an assessment grid which compares the three future scenarios under three headings: Economic sustainability, Social sustainability, Environmental sustainability. Which scenario do you think promises the best urban future?

SECTION D

A gloomy prospect

The processes and directions of change discussed in the previous section will not be the only ones to affect urbanisation in the 21st century. Almost certainly there will be others. With the one prospect of cities as we know them dispersing into some other, much looser form of urban growth, it is perhaps appropriate to remind ourselves of some of the advantages that compact cities have to offer (**7.2**). Perhaps in earlier chapters we have dwelt too much on their disadvantages.

Perhaps the single greatest barrier to achieving sustainable urban development (**7.1**) and maximising the plus points of the city (**7.2**) is the lack of good governance. **Good governance** may be defined as having the right institutional structure to do the job. Having democratic and uncorrupted government at city, regional and national levels is a vital part, but not all of it. The ethics of honesty and openness need to apply to all the urban managers (**3.3**). *Dialogue*, *partnership* and *co-operation* are key action words.

Figure 7.2 The positive sides to the city

* High densities mean much lower costs per household and per enterprise for the provision of:
  - piped, treated water supplies
  - collection and disposal of wastes
  - advanced telecommunications
  - health care and education.

* High densities mean a reduced demand for land relative to population.

* Cities provide a concentration of production and consumption. This means a stronger possibility of resources being used efficiently.

* In climates where homes and businesses need to be heated for all or part of the year, concentration offers potential for reducing the use of fossil fuels.

* Cities offer a much greater potential for limiting the use of motor vehicles.

* Cities are important cradles and expressions of culture.

* Cities have strong social economies – voluntary actions that strengthen the sense of neighbourhood and community.

The possible future scenarios that we have briefly glimpsed in this chapter do not seem to offer any real prospect of sustainable urban development. Let us not forget that unsustainable urbanisation promises unsustainable cities. Unsustainable cities in turn promise a troubled world. A dispersing urban world driven by advances in transport and communication means further erosion and dilution of rural space and a possible discard of the city as we know it. Sadly, that is the way the future of the urban world looks today. Let's hope I am proved wrong!

Further reading

J. Brotchie *et al.* (eds), *Cities of the Twenty-First Century*, Longman, 1991.

A. Champion and C. Watkins (eds), *People in the Countryside*, Paul Chapman, 1991.

A. J. Fielding, 'Counterurbanisation: threat or blessing?' in D. Pinder (ed.), *Western Europe: Challenge and Change*, Belhaven, 1990.

S. Graham and S. Marvin, *Telecommunications and the City*, Routledge, 1996.

T. Hall, *Urban Geography*, Routledge, 1998.

G. Haughton and C. Hunter, *Sustainable Cities*, Jessica Kingsley, 1994.

R. Imrie and H. Thomas (eds), *British Urban Policy and the Urban Development Corporations*, Paul Chapman, 1995.

P. L. Knox, *The Restless Urban Landscape*, Prentice-Hall, 1993.

P. L. Knox and J. Agnew, *The Geography of the World Economy*, Edward Arnold, 1995.

P. L. Knox and P. J. Taylor (eds), *World Cities in a World System*, CUP, 1985.

S. Page, *Urban Tourism*, Routledge, 1996.

R. Potter, *Urbanisation in the Third World*, OUP, 1992.

J. L. Shurmer-Smith and D. Burtenshaw, 'Urban decay and rejuvenation' in D. Pinder (ed.), *Western Europe: Challenge and Change*, Belhaven, 1990.

UN Centre for Human Settlements, *An Urbanizing World: Global Report on Human Settlements*, OUP, 1996.